DRY STONE WALLING

TECHNIQUES & TRADITIONS

Wall the Best

John Shaw Rimington

The
Dry Stone Walling Association
of Great Britain

Published and produced by the
Dry Stone Walling Association of Great Britain
Westmorland County Showground,
Lane Farm, Crooklands,
Milnthorpe, Cumbria LA7 7NH
www.dswa.org.uk

First edition, published 2004.

The Association publishes a range of books and leaflets.
Full details available on request or from the website.

The DSWA is a registered charity.
All proceeds from the sale of this book are used to further the objectives of the Association.
Charity registration number: 289678

British Library Cataloguing in Publication Data: a catalogue record of this book is available from the British Library.

© DSWA, 2004

Printed in England by G W Belton Limited, Gainsborough.

ISBN: 0 9512306 8 9

The Association gratefully acknowledges the
Department for Environment, Food and Rural Affairs for
financial support from the Rural Enterprise Scheme which has
enabled production of this book.

This project has been supported under the Rural Enterprise Scheme

CONTENTS

ACKNOWLEDGEMENTS

Paul Webley, on behalf of the Dry Stone Walling Association of Great Britain, has compiled this publication : the DSWA holds copyright of this original work. The Association holds the full copyright of this published edition.

The Association wishes to acknowledge the work of members and supporters who have contributed specifically to this book, which has been based on a format developed originally by Richard Tufnell in a series of booklets written for the Association. In alphabetical order we acknowledge:

John R Bown	Philip Clark	Kenneth France
Dave Goulder	David Griffiths	George Gunn
Norman Haddow	Brenda Koo	Andrew Loudon
Richard Love	William F Noble	Margaret Ribchester
Neil Rippingale	James Scott	Christopher Stephens
Carolyn Murray-Wooley	Trevor F Wragg	

The following titles have been taken out of print as their subject matter is expanded in this single publication:
Building Special Features in Dry Stone
Better Dry Stone Walling
Creating a Natural Stone Garden – Inspirational Ideas for Gardens

The Association wishes to acknowledge the work of members and supporters who contributed to the titles mentioned above, especially Richard Tufnell whose original work (of which he holds copyright) enabled the Association to develop the booklets. Others to whom thanks are due are (in alphabetical order):

Ian K Dewar	Alan W Hill	Margaret Ribchester
Jacqui Simkins	Richard Tufnell	Paul Webley

The drawings used in this publication include some of those commissioned by the Association for its previously published books and specification leaflets. The photographs have been kindly provided by members and supporters. DSWA acknowledges:

Sean Adcock	Bridget Flemming	Janet Gaskell
William Holmes	S Huguet	Brian K Jones
Carol Lewis	Andrew Loudon	Margaret Ribchester
John Riddick	Jacqui Simkins	Christopher Stephens
Richard Tufnell	Paul Webley	Trevor Wragg
	and others	

Special thanks go to Margaret Ribchester for her publishing skills and advice; and to Jacqui Simkins, who has waded through numerous drafts and has acted as editor. Without her help and encouragement this book would never have been completed.

INTRODUCTION

In compiling this book, the Association has tried to draw together much of the knowledge lying in the experienced hands of its craftsmen around the country. This publication is not an attempt to cover every topic or type and style of walling, but to give an insight into the use of dry stone at the present time. The craft has changed considerably over the last thirty years, moving from a base in agriculture to become firmly established both in decorative horticulture and in the field of public arts. While wallers and dykers still rely on agricultural work for the basis of their living, there is increasing demand for them to create many of the features explained in this book and it is therefore important to include them.

The more complex features need to be constructed by experienced hands: they are certainly not for the beginner.

FOREWORD

Dry stone walls are found throughout the British Isles, particularly in the upland areas. They also occur in many other countries; wherever stone is found on or near the surface of the ground, it has been used for building dwellings and enclosing fields. Throughout recorded history, developing civilizations have used stone both in its natural state and after dressing or shaping.

Dry stone masonry techniques have been used to build a variety of structures throughout the world. The techniques from the past continue to be appropriate in modern day walling and have been adapted for use on a huge variety of stone types.

The earliest known example of dry stone walling in the British Isles dates from 3200 BC; it lies at Skara Brae in the Orkneys. A complete settlement has been unearthed, including houses and other buildings made from stone which has received minimal dressing. Doorways, hearths, beds and seats as well as freestanding walls were constructed here using stone that was sorted and carefully chosen for its purpose. The methods of placing and tying stone together are very similar to those used in the present day. Other early buildings survive, for example on the Dingle peninsula in western Ireland.

While these methods have obviously been known and used during the last five millennia , there is over most of Britain little surviving evidence of what was built for most of that time. Around 1200 walls began to appear as boundaries for the great sheep ranges owned and run by the monasteries. These were constructed with the additional purpose of clearing the fields of loose-lying stones, and were massively built though with little refinement of technique. They consisted of wide, high walls of simply piled stone that ran for miles with no concession to any steep slopes. These long lines of piled-up stone became the earliest form of dry stone field boundary.

Early walls also appeared around settlements, often as a result of the clearance of stone to allow crops to be grown on the land. As livestock numbers increased, some small fields were created to provide safe refuge close to settlements: these enabled their owners to provide shelter for their animals to keep them safe from predators or thieves. As more land was improved for grazing, walls became useful to stop livestock straying and to ensure that the grazing was efficiently managed. It is only in modern times that dry stone work has been used within gardens or in a purely decorative manner.

CHARACTERISTICS OF DRY STONE WALLS

The strength of a dry stone wall lies in the careful positioning of its stones to make full use of their weight and of the friction between their surfaces. Walls may be built either as single-skinned structures, where the stone is large and rough, or as double-skinned walls with an inner core of broken stone: both types of construction are covered in this book.

Regional styles evolved to make best use of the stone found in each locality and have been refined over the centuries to produce walls with characteristics distinctive to their local areas. Despite differing stone types, the basic techniques of the craft have remained the same.

In this book we will firstly address the techniques, then relate them to the commonly observed field walls and to the more creative recent developments in the use of dry stone walling.

SKILLS

Anyone can achieve a basic level of skill in this craft; but to reach the proficiency attained by the best professionals takes years of practice, combined with a continuous critical analysis of each completed piece of work in search of continuing self-improvement.

Every new wall presents a fresh challenge and is the ultimate problem-solving exercise. Each stone placed should solve a problem, and do so without creating another one.

True craftsmen of both past and present take a pride in their work - work that will stand for generations. They are always aware that others will critically examine what they do. The present generation of craftsmen has plenty of good examples from past years to emulate, and the reader is urged to look carefully at the styles and compare the quality of work in his or her own area.

STONE

Dry stone walls use a great deal of stone: one tonne of stone will build about one square metre of free-standing wall, though more is needed for thicker or higher walls. Sourcing stone can be both time-consuming and expensive, but with a little thought this can be minimised. Stone should be moved the shortest distance possible, as transport can be a major cost.

Buying new stone from quarries can be the most expensive option, and few quarries are accustomed to supplying the needs of the dry stone waller. Changes in farming practices leave old, derelict field walls that may be a useful source of stone. Disused quarries are also a possibility, but a word of warning: always check with landowners and local authority before taking stone from any source, even though purchase may have been agreed. Surface stone in some areas is protected and, even if loose, must not be collected.

The Dry Stone Walling Association publishes an annual Register of Certificated Professional Members and Sources of Stone, which would be a good starting point. Directories such as Yellow Pages contain a section incorporating quarries (in this case all quarries, not simply those supplying walling stone) and there are a number of directories of stone types and stone quarries which may be available in local libraries produced by organisations such as The Stone Federation and by a number of commercial publishing houses. Many professional wallers can also recommend local stone suppliers.

WALLING WORDS

In common with many crafts, dry stone walling has developed its own vocabulary of words and phrases. The glossary at the back of this book will provide a translation of walling terminology.

BASIC TECHNIQUES

TOOLS AND EQUIPMENT

The tools needed to build dry stone walls are few and of modest cost. It is only in the case of difficult sites where large amounts of material have to be moved that anything mechanical is necessary.

A measure
Two building lines
  (if attached to pins they are easier to use)
Pickaxe or mattock
Spade or shovel
Crowbar
A couple of hammers
  (weighing between 1 and 2 kilos)
Sledgehammer
A personal first aid kit should always be with you when working.

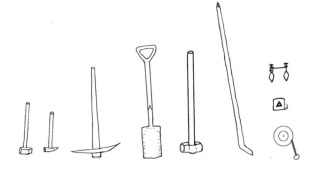

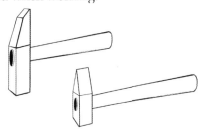

Hammer styles and weights vary from area to area: a Scottish type and a Pennine style are illustrated here.

Sometimes a wheelbarrow is useful for moving soil away and hauling stone to where you want it. A heavy-duty bucket is essential for collecting small stones together for packing the centre of the wall. When working with very large stone, some wallers use sack trucks.

Professional wallers often make use of four pieces of reinforcement bar (rebar) some 1800mm in length, or four road irons, to mark out the line and batter of the wall. An alternative is to make up two walling frames or templates (illustrated) from pieces of wood to the precise dimensions of the wall to be built. The uprights on these frames need to be quite strong and it is suggested you use wood of at least 80mm x 40mm. The top horizontal is usually set at the height of the top of the coursed wall, the level at which you put on the copes. Some walls are constructed with less slope (batter) on one side than the other and in these cases a walling frame is particularly useful.

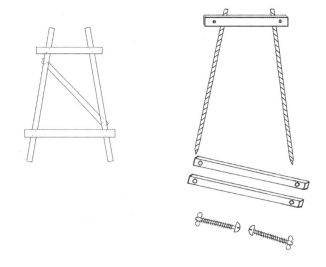

Where you are rebuilding a large gap, the sound wall to either side will provide a shape to follow. Lines can be set across the gap, pinned into joints of the standing wall at either side. They should be stretched parallel to the ground and each other and raised as you build.

In the case of a new wall, you have to set up a template. This can be in the form of a frame held in place by a walling iron, or bars hammered into the ground to create the shape and hold the lines horizontally at the correct distance apart to create the batter of the wall. The lines can be tied around the inside of the frame or bar and raised as work progresses. Make sure lines are always tight or you may end up with a wavering wall.

SAFETY

Many wallers have been injured by not taking safety issues seriously. When you break stone it splinters and can do great damage. You should always wear protective goggles or safety glasses and be particularly aware of the potential danger to people or objects nearby.

Even professional wallers wear strong gloves much of the time to gain some protection from squashing or pinching of the fingers and help to prevent abrasions. There is a very real risk of injury from rusty nails, staples and broken glass when stripping out old walls, so it is as well to be sure that your tetanus jabs are up to date. Infections such as Leptospirosis & Weil's Disease can be contracted from rodent nests, etc., so always wash thoroughly before eating and drinking. And do not underestimate the damage that handling stone can do to the skin; many a waller has dropped hot tea or coffee as a result of developing very tender, thin-skinned finger tips!

Feet, and especially toes, need protection too. Falling stones can inflict painful damage. Boots with reinforced toecaps are essential, and it is as well to lace them tightly to help prevent sprained ankles.

Over half of all injuries to working wallers are caused either by incorrect lifting or by tripping or falling over stones. In order to avoid back injuries, always lift stones by holding them close to the body, bending the legs and keeping the back straight. Slide or walk heavy stones up a plank and always be realistic about your limitations; get help where necessary. You will greatly reduce your chance of standing on a forgotten stone if you keep the strip of ground near the wall clear, and resist the temptation to walk backwards to get a better view of your work.

There is a need to take particular care when working alongside roads. Some local authorities require only qualified persons to set up safety zones with signs and cones, as these must conform to the Traffic Signs Regulations in force at the time that the work is to be carried out. A booklet is available from HMSO bookshops explaining these (see *Further reading*).

BUILDING THE WALL

There is no single style for building dry stone walls. Styles vary depending on the stone and the local tradition. The wall described here is a stock proof 1.4 metre high wall of a type that can be seen in many areas. Dimensions can be varied to allow for walls of different heights, but over generations it has been found that the base width should be twice the width of the wall measured immediately beneath the copestones. By adding these two widths together you can get an approximate measure of the height of the wall before the cope is put on.

USING THE RIGHT STONE IN THE RIGHT PLACE

If you are dismantling an old wall it is important to organise the stone. Separate the types and sizes of stone and place them in different piles, far enough apart to ensure they are not mixed together. If you are working with newly quarried stone, or stone that has been tipped in one big pile, it is important before starting work to sort it into sizes for best use in the correct parts of the wall. Stand the stones on end so that the best face is visible: this will save much time when you come to build.

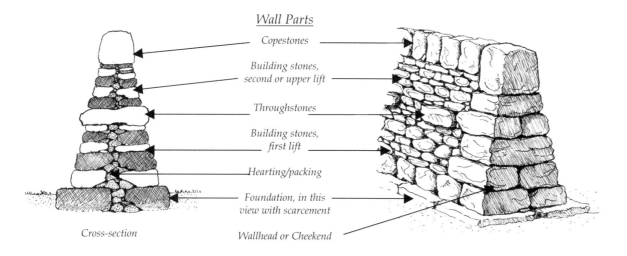

Wall Parts

Copestones

Building stones, second or upper lift

Throughstones

Building stones, first lift

Hearting/packing

Foundation, in this view with scarcement

Cross-section

Wallhead or Cheekend

Stones can be used in six ways in a wall, and every scrap will have its place.

1. <u>Foundation stones</u>: large, heavy stones, sometimes irregularly shaped, capable of bearing the full weight of the wall.

2. <u>Building stones</u>: stones used to build the two outer faces or skins of the wall. They can be of varying thickness, but the larger and thicker they are the lower they should be placed in the wall.

3. <u>Throughstones</u>: these are stones that run right through the wall to tie the two skins together. They are hard to find, and should be handled carefully and NEVER broken up.

4. <u>Copestones</u>: these sit tightly locked together on top of the wall and their weight bears downwards and ties the wall together. Their shape varies from area to area, but they should be wide enough to bridge the top of the wall and be about 20-30 cm. high. These stones should be picked out and put firmly to one side, since it can be tempting to use them as building stones.

5. <u>Hearting or packing</u>: small pieces of stone, or broken stone, CAREFULLY placed to pack the middle of the wall between the two faces and support the inner length of the building stones.

6. <u>Pins or pinnings</u>: small, tapering pieces of stone used to lock the row of copestones together or to wedge face stones from the back so that they lie level.

STRIPPING OUT

If you are to restore an old wall, or have to transport stone from a wall to build elsewhere, it is good practice to note how it was originally used. Careful examination of how an old wall was put together will aid you in rebuilding it. It may also help you to avoid the faults which made it collapse, such as straight joints, inadequate batter, poor tying in or support of stones, lack of throughstones etc. If you are gapping, it will be sensible to ensure that the wall into which you are tying is sound.

The first step in stripping out an old wall is to lift off the copestones one at a time. If these are heavy, brace your body against the wall, hold a stone close to you, turn and carry it to place with the others in a straight line two to three metres away from where the wall is to be rebuilt.

The next stage is to take down the two faces of the wall, distributing the stone equally on both sides of the construction line. It is easiest to place the stones from each skin or face on the side they came from, but it is useful to even out the old stone when additional new material is to be added. Leave a clear working space of at least 60 cm along each side of the wall and place stones on edge, best face upwards.

All the small hearting stones should be placed in piles fairly close to the wall, beside the building stones, retaining a clear workspace.

The throughstones should be carefully laid out (not dropped or thrown!) on the opposite side of the wall to the copestones, some two to three metres away.

Foundation stones are often well bedded into the ground. If you are rebuilding and the foundations are in line and not sloping outwards, they may be left. If you have to take them out, it is unwise to move them too far since they are heavy, and in any case they will soon be used in the rebuilding.

FOUNDATIONS

If you are building a new wall, mark out and dig a shallow trench a few centimetres wider than the base of the wall, removing all topsoil, roots and vegetation and depositing them some distance away. Stamp the subsoil down well so that it is firm. If the ground is stony this is not necessary, but a shallow trench is essential as it stops the foundation stones from spreading.

Set strings or lines just wider than the wall base, so as to allow a little room outside the foundation stones for adjustment. In some areas the foundation layer is stepped out wider than the first building course, but it is always advisable to work to the characteristics of your local area. Where the underlying ground is soft, however, a wider foundation makes for slower and more even settling of the wall.

The foundation stones should be large and should be placed with a good face outwards, almost touching the guide lines, and with the flattest surface uppermost. An irregular surface can be bedded into the base of the trench. Make sure that the stones reach well into the centre of the wall. Where possible, make sure that the stones touch each other at the face and that they are laid as level as possible.

Stones should not be laid as triangles with their points inwards as this can result in gaps appearing near the edges, especially if the first building course is stepped in from a wider foundation.

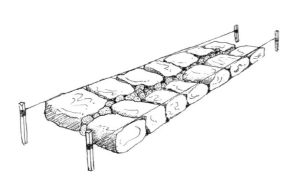

When foundation stones are in line on both sides of a reasonable length of your wall, level them up using wedges or pins inserted <u>from the middle towards the outside of the wall</u>, making the wedges as large as possible. The space between the two lines of foundation stones should be carefully packed so that nothing will move. Try to achieve an effect like paving with a good flat surface on which to build the next course. Never toss the hearting in – each piece has a role to play in supporting its neighbours. The firmness of foundation stones can be tested by standing on them to see if they move: if they do, work the wedges until all are firm.

Dry stone walls should not be built on a concrete base, as this prevents the wall from settling and thus from tightening properly.

BUILDING THE FIRST LIFT (foundation to throughstones)
Throughout the work it is worth considering a few guidelines which will help you build a tighter, stronger wall.

1. If you are building a coursed wall, always try to choose stones that will sit side by side without a change of level. A step between differing heights will act as a knife-edge and the weight above will crack the stone placed across this edge. When building in a random style, you need to guard against the development of diagonally running joints across the face of the wall.

2. In the lower levels of the wall, use stones with a good outside face; but also make sure they have enough length running <u>into</u> the wall so that the two opposite face stones take up most of the width. It takes more time to select these stones but their use makes the wall much stronger.

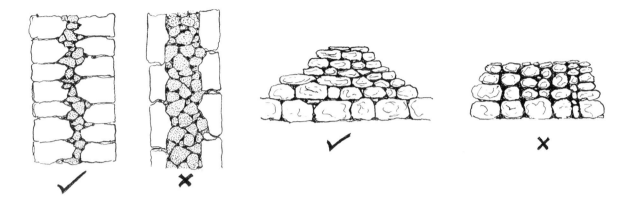

3.   Always cover with one stone the joint formed by two touching stones below it. You will form a series of inverted 'T' shapes throughout the wall. This is often called 'two on one and one on two'.

4.   Use your largest building stones in the lower half of the wall. They can best bear the weight above them and often have greatest reach into the wall. Conversely, smaller stone is often shorter into the wall, and this is best placed higher up where the wall is narrower.

5.   Work methodically, making sure each stone is wedged firmly in place before moving to the next. Try to work along the line, placing each stone in turn. Do not leave gaps between stones; it takes a lot of time to find a stone that fits a gap.

6.   Place each stone gently. They do not fit any better if you bang them down or hit them, and such treatment can loosen lower stones. If you hear stone hit the wall hard, then it is not being properly placed.

7.   Pack the wall, completing each course as you go. If you keep the hearting a little high between the courses, it can often provide a handy source of pinnings to support a stone you are laying in the next course.

8.   Build up both sides of the wall at the same rate, keeping each at the same height. Never build several courses on one side and then bring the other up to match: this leaves the first side vulnerable and makes good packing almost impossible.

9.   Bring the lines up as you work, and keep the faces of the stones almost touching the lines. This will result in a good, even batter to the wall. Keep your courses running horizontally where possible.

Using these principles the work of building the wall should continue up to half its final height (measured from the base to below the copestones). At this point it should be carefully levelled off and the centre tightly packed. You are now ready to place the throughstones.

THROUGHSTONES

Throughstones are placed about halfway up the wall and bind the faces together. In the case of a wall of 1.4m high excluding copes, throughstones are placed at 0.55cm, or about knee level on a man of average height.

Ideally throughstones should be placed no more than one metre apart, measured centre to centre. They bridge the half-built wall, often projecting a little on each side (sometimes the local style may project on one side only, or not at all). These stones may need to be cut to fit or their position in the wall must be chosen to allow for their length, i.e. the shorter they are, the higher they are placed. When insufficient throughs are available, three-quarter length stones (frequently called three-quarter throughs and occasionally called galf stones) are placed so that their tails overlap in the centre of the wall: these must be placed so that they are on different courses with their inner sections pressing against each other. If placed side-by-side, three-quarter throughs have no contact friction created to make them grip each other so they do not prevent the wall's two faces from moving apart.

If throughstones protrude too far, animals use them to scratch. Cattle scratching up and down can move an over-long throughstone and loosen the whole top half of a wall.

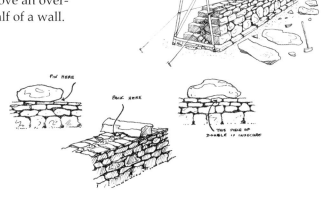

Place the throughstones on the wall so that they cover the joints in the course below on both faces. Lay them gently and carefully. You often need a helper to move these large stones. Throughstones should be well supported under the centre with hearting or wedges to prevent them from cracking under the weight of the wall above.

Raise the lines or string to the top of the throughstones and continue building until you have filled the gaps and the wall is level.

SECOND LIFT

On the first course of the second lift, it is important to cross the joints above each throughstone, to prevent a vertical joint from developing at this crucial place. The wall gradually becomes narrower and the smaller building stones are now used. As smaller stones are lighter, even more care is needed in securing them. This part of the wall should be finished level at its final height below copestone level.

COVERBAND

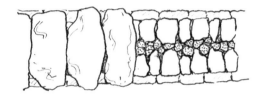

Coverband stones being laid on top of the "double"

In some areas the wall is levelled off with a coverband of wide, flat stones. This is more common in sandstone areas where suitable small flags are easy to find. Coverband stones need to be placed so that they do not rock and must be packed well underneath to trap every stone in the top course.

COPESTONES

The wall will now measure about 35cm wide - half the width it did at its base. You are ready to set the copestones in place. The wisdom of having sorted these out and left them alone should now be evident.

Having carefully assessed the average height of your available material, choose large, solid copestones and place one at each end of the section that you have built to mark the height that you intend for your finished coping. Run a line between these as a means of making sure the finished wall has a straight and level top. It may be necessary to put another copestone at the halfway point to prevent the line from sagging.

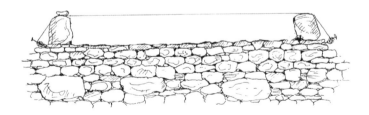

Lines set for copes

Set each copestone so that it almost touches the line. Copestones should be chosen to fit tightly to each other. Where the copestones are too low, individual stones can be placed on a suitable thickness of flat stone to raise them a little. Stones which are too large can be carefully dressed to the correct height.

The final stage is to pin the copestones by tapping wedges of a suitable size down vertically between them. Knock in each wedge in turn a little at a time, and work along the row to keep the integrity of the whole line: if you knock wedges in completely one after the other, the copes may move or twist.

If you have done this correctly you will now have a cope with all stones locked as tightly as if they had been bedded in concrete! Never check for solidity by walking along the top of the wall: this is unnecessary and dangerous and besides, walls are not footpaths. The correct way to check is to attempt to rock each stone in turn, working along the wall until you know the whole section is solid.

There are regional variations as to how copes are placed; some areas use vertical copes, while others place them at an angle.

Copes vary from region to region, always try to match the style of the locality

The types of copings placed on walls often vary quite widely within a small locality. In some areas large flags are used as copes, in others double lines of smaller stones or even a turf top may be employed. The aim, however, is to add weight to the top of the wall, pressing all lower courses tightly together and binding the top throughout the length of the wall. Always follow the style of other copestones in the immediate vicinity.

Where there is no coverband, copestones should be wide enough to sit with their bases flat and right across the top of the wall, tying both faces together. Any convex projection in the middle of the base must be removed with the hammer to ensure that the copestone does not rock.

All that is left to do is to tidy that part of the site and move any surplus stones along to your next working area.

WALLHEADS AND CHEEKENDS

Most free-standing walls end in a wallhead: the only exceptions might be if the site calls for them to taper to meet rising ground or for some other practical reason. They are the most common feature found in walling, being built to stop walls at gateways or to provide gaps for access.

Mastering the building of wallheads is essential before a waller can move on to other features, since the techniques used are also needed in the building of lunkies, some stiles, some types of arch, for pillars and for strengthening long walls on steeply sloping ground. Where a gatepost is to be put in against a wallhead, it is best to dig the hole and secure the post in its final position before the wall is built: concrete or well-rammed stone is used to fill the hole. A completely solid fill is needed or soil will move from under the foundation stones at the wallhead, causing it to lean over towards the post.

A wall is normally constructed with a wallhead as shown in the diagram. The walling frame is made to fit against the end of the wall or gatepost and set so that both sides taper by an equal amount (if the wall has similar batter on both sides).

The wallhead should be built with long stones resembling throughstones and each course should be constructed at the same time as the related course in the main wall. Stones are placed alternately so that they lie across the end of the wall on one course and, at the next, run into its length. It is essential that a vertical joint does not develop up the end of the wall and that the stones which run along the faces do not form a vertical joint adjacent to the wallhead. These weaknesses would allow the head to break open or to break away from the main wall

Doubled wallhead for a wall with a scarcement

The two foundation stones of the wallhead should be large and tie well into the wall running lengthways. It is sometimes necessary to add a third stone between the two base stones to fill the whole width. All these stones should be set as level as possible across their top surfaces as they are going to be crossed with a throughstone to act as the first stone on the next course. Starting from these stones, the first course of the wall should be built working away from the wallhead. The second course starts with a throughstone across its width which should be trimmed to follow the batter and should not be more than half the length of the longer foundation stones, so that joints can be well crossed and trace walling is avoided. This through should be well packed with hearting, and the rest of this course should then be built working away from the head.

The third course is built as was the first, with the length of the corner stones placed along the wall; again, a third stone may be needed if these two are not large enough to touch at the head.

In most cases wallheads are built with large stones but many competent wallers use smaller material, believing that the more stone surfaces there are to bind with each other, the stronger the result. Whichever method is used, it is essential to sort out the most appropriate stones for it at the start. It is also wise to be stone rich – to have more stone than you need - as any use of the hammer in dressing the pieces risks breakage, which might render a stone unusable in its intended position.

As in the rest of your work, attention should be paid to proper packing, and to ensuring that large stones are well seated on each other. The end-stone must be very large, square and able to resist the pressure of the copes behind it. Building a good, strong wallhead takes time and patience.

REBUILDING A GAP

This is perhaps the most convenient way for a beginner to gain experience. Almost all the necessary stone is likely to be nearby from the wall's collapse, although experience will show that in carrying out any rebuild additional stone is useful. The line of the wall already exists and the style of walling can be matched.

When rebuilding a gap, ensure there is sound wall at either side into which your work may be tied. Start the process by sorting and laying out the fallen stone; this may be difficult if the section has been down for a season or two as soil and vegetation may have covered much of the stone. Working around the base of the wall gently with the point of a pickaxe may unearth buried treasures.

Next, remove any loose stone from the standing wall. The good wall on each side of the gap must be racked back (stepped) to enable the rebuild to take place without vertical joints being created at each end of the repair. It is a good idea at this point to check your supply of copestones and ensure they are placed away from the main stock.

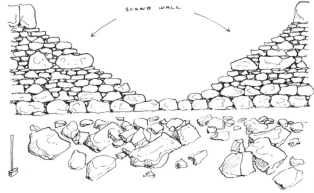

Finally, before starting to replace stone, check the foundations. If any foundation stones have tilted or are out of line they should be removed and correctly relaid; such movement is a common cause of failure in dry stone walls, and underlines the importance of laying these stones on a good solid base.

Lay out your stone correctly when repairing any wall or gap – if will save you time and effort

In rebuilding a gap, walling frames or irons are unnecessary as the line pins can be pushed between stones in the sound wall so that your lines can be stretched tightly between them. Wall each course on each face in turn, pack the centre of the wall, then raise the lines as you go, ensuring that you cover every joint until you reach the level of the throughs. Place your throughstones by referring to the existing ones in the sound wall for positioning, and then continue building to the level of the copes.

At this stage, if you have been disciplined and not plundered your copes for the body of the wall, all you should be left with is the correct number of copes with which to finish it. If the adjacent style is sloping, start replacing them from the end at which they lean away from the gap. If the ground slopes but the copes are vertical, start at the lower end and work uphill.

CORNERS

While a template for the shape of a wallhead can be modelled on a walling frame, a corner presents a more complex problem.

In the main, the binding or tying in technique is similar to that used in constructing a wallhead. The long stones are interlocked like the teeth of a zip with stones running in alternate directions along the wall.

Remember, however, that each face has its own batter, and therefore the points at which the faces meet draw more closely together as the wall grows taller. There is no vertical face on a corner. The best way to prepare for this is to set up two walling frames at the correct angle to each other, at a short distance from the corner to be built. These set the profile of the two individual walls. Set another pair of frames at a suitable distance along the line of each of the two walls. These will be moved away from the corner as the walls extend. Use two lines to each frame, raising each line to the top of each new corner stone as it is laid.

The stones that make the inner corner interlock in the same way as the ones on the outer. If you fail to raise each line before setting the next stone the opposite way, it will trap one of the lines. Once again, build away from the corner stones, course by course, as described in the wallhead section, levelling each course with well-placed packing.

Having the walling frames a short distance away from each face allows you to sight along the wall regularly, ensuring that no vertical joints are developing in the faces close to the corner. Once the lines have been taken away, check that no stones offend the eye and the rhythm of building in the rest of the wall is maintained.

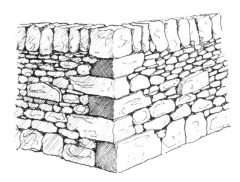

Right angled corner: make best use of the stone available

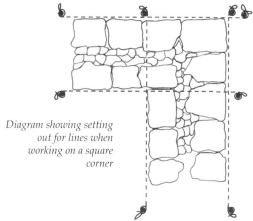

Diagram showing setting out for lines when working on a square corner

When placing copes on a corner, start by selecting a copestone which is large and square and has enough weight to sit firmly and will not move under the pressure which will bear on it from both sides. Sometimes it is necessary to find several matching copes to sit at the corner, so that the ones that run away from these will fit neatly to each other without twisting.

WALLS ON SLOPING GROUND

These can be quite difficult to build: everything, including the wall, tends to slide downhill at every opportunity and the aim is to prevent the stone from doing the same once the wall is built.

On very shallow slopes, gravity poses little problem and the stone can be allowed to run with the ground, but where the slope is steeper, and particularly if the stone is flattish and offers little friction, this cannot be considered good practice.

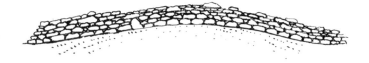

Wall being built on gently undulating ground

Once the slope reaches twenty degrees or more, and on shallower slopes with material of low frictional properties, the foundations and subsequent courses must be laid horizontally and the wall built upwards from the bottom of the slope.

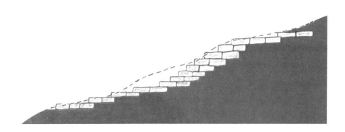

Stepped foundations dug out and laid with horizontal courses

To achieve this, a shallow horizontal foundation trench is dug into the slope until the subsoil is just to the top of the height of the first stones selected for the foundation course. The trench is stepped and the next level will be at the top of that stone, being dug back horizontally into the slope in the same manner. The steeper the slope, the shorter each trench length will be. As each subsequent group of foundation stones is laid, half a stone overlaps the one below at the step.

You are now ready to build the body of the wall, starting with a strong wallhead – very strong - at the bottom of the slope. You will soon realise there is a problem with setting lines when building on sloping ground: the lines will appear to widen as they go with the slope. This is because a single course which begins say half way up the wallhead will run horizontally into the slope and at the same time will get nearer to the wall base as the ground rises; so eventually this course will lead into the foundation. (Read this sentence twice.)

In fact the point may arise when your lines run horizontally from just beneath the cope to the foundation at ground level (remember the rule of thumb: the lines will be approximately twice the width apart at the foundation as they are beneath the cope). Many wallers who regularly rebuild walls on steep slopes use a second set of lines, set to run with the slope and to maintain a constant distance apart. Following such lines ensures that no bulges develop and that throughstones are placed at the correct height above ground.

Finally, it is as well to note the following points about safe, careful working:
1.   It is always easier to move stone down rather than up a slope. In fact many old hill walls used stones from small quarries higher up the slope on which they stood.
2.   More accidents occur on slopes than anywhere else. If the soil is wet it becomes dangerous as both you and your stone can easily slip.
3.   Never work lower down the slope than another waller on the same side of the wall – you are in an avalanche zone. It is always worth banging in a few lengths of rebar and putting up a couple of scaffold planks to prevent any escaping stones from rolling all the way to the bottom. This structure can be easily moved up the slope as you complete each section of wall.

There has been much debate over the years on the subject of topping off on sloping ground, and professional wallers seem fairly equally divided in their opinions as to whether to start putting on the copestones at the bottom of the slope or at the top. Similarly, some wallers say copes should lean uphill, some say downhill, and some say they should be vertical.

As the wall is built from the bottom of the slope, it is easier to start to cope from there and to set the first one against a good heavy end-stone which will prevent the whole lot from slipping. You then work away from it, following the steps in the top course or the slope in the coverband.

Wall on steep slope with horizontal courses showing stepped foundation

It is more sensible to top each section as you work, and that means starting at the bottom of the slope and working uphill. In this way, you tidy as you go and work gradually up on to drier, less trodden and less slippery ground. Whatever the local style, if the copes are well placed, they will be self-trapping.

When topping off, the line of the copestones needs to be sympathetic to the slope of the ground. There should be no sudden changes of height. One master craftsman uses the term 'sweetening the tops'. However it is described, the final line of the top of the wall should flow evenly up and down slopes and should look natural to the eye.

Check that all copes are tight. Tap in wedges if necessary as described previously. Gently attempt to move each stone: re-wedge where you feel any movement. NEVER check for solidity by walking along the top of the wall.

RETAINING WALLS
Retaining walls are built where there is a substantial difference in ground level between two sides of a wall. They are used to form terracing, to counteract soil slump on hills and to prevent erosion by water. In some parts of the world, whole mountainsides are terraced. In addition, retaining walls are found lining sunken lanes and at times cladding the sides of watercourses. Retaining walls can also serve a dual purpose within a garden since as well as forming part of a whole series of good features they provide a marvellous habitat for trailing or climbing plants.

As this type of wall is subjected to potentially large pressure both downward and from the back, it is important to bear in mind that weight in the wall helps retain weight; a thin, lightweight wall will have no resistance to the pressures involved.

LOW RETAINING WALLS
If you are working across a slope to form a terrace, cut the bank back to allow sufficient space to build the wall. There must be enough room both to build and to fill the space behind with stone. As you dig, save any suitable stone for hearting or backfilling. If the soil is crumbly or unstable, it is a good idea to dig back an extra 15cm to allow for soil falling in as you build. Place the soil that you dig out on the bank above, ready to use later for backfilling or levelling.

Although you can, if you wish, build a standard double-skinned wall, this is not always necessary. It is sufficient to build the outer face only, packing behind it carefully as you go. This method requires fewer good face stones, is quicker to build, and requires only one building line. If the wall is to be higher than 60cm or so, remember you will need throughstones running inwards at the usual spacing. Do not leave them insufficiently supported at the back; you may need more packing, and if the throughs tie back into the bank behind, then so much the better. Throughstones should not project too far out of the face: if you cannot set them further back, dig out behind them.

It looks most impressive to have two or more terraces, one above the other. Make sure the foundations of the upper walls are not placed on soil loosened and excavated for the wall below. Plan not only the order in which you intend to build them, but also the placing of the stone, before you start.

You will need suitable stones to build a wallhead at each end, unless you are lucky enough to be able to tie into a bank. Dry stone walls drain well but should water be a real problem, you may have to dig a drain or incorporate a smoot to allow it to pass harmlessly away. As long as you have sufficient stone available, there should be no need to fit poorly shaped stones into the face of the wall; use them in the back. Finally, finish the project by shovelling the waste behind the wall and levelling off with good soil.

HIGH RETAINING WALLS
Two different techniques have been adopted to build high retaining walls in the UK. In the first, the wall is built in a similar manner to a free-standing field wall but with a batter of close to 1-in-6 rather than the usual 1-in-8.

These walls are built with a strong but rough back face which uses the poorer shaped stones, and as many throughstones are put in as possible. These are placed in rows as the wall rises, usually staggered on alternate rows (as opposite).

The other method employed in some areas does away with the back face altogether and instead uses a lot of heavy packing between the front face and the soil or rubble that is being retained.

Whichever method is used, if the tails of the throughs are not bedded into the bank behind they need to be very well supported. If this is not achieved a through will settle over time; outward pressure below it will create a bulge in the wall, while the inward pulling motion above will tend to create a dish.

In areas which experience a lot of rainfall - and most of the hilly areas of Britain come into this category - it is often essential to provide drainage at the wall base. If either the front or back foundation lies constantly in mud, the soil may deform like Plasticine and be squeezed out between the stones. When this happens evenly along the wall, a steady settling takes place, but if one section of the wall lies wetter than the rest the foundations here may settle more quickly and the whole section may slump. In extreme cases, a drain should run along the back of the wall to carry the water away. Do not excavate the drain at the front of the wall; a ditch deeper than the foundations will allow the lower courses to move forward and result in a collapse of the back of the wall.

In some areas walls are built across slopes to arrest soil creep and at the same time to retain livestock. In this case a normal free-standing field wall is built, sometimes incorporating a base that is wider than usual. Should you need to build a wall of this type where the soil backfill only reaches part way up the field wall, it will be wise to incorporate regular weep holes at this level. The ideal place for these is above large, flattish throughs that have their upper surface just above the level of the soil at the rear. In times of heavy rain, any water that might have flooded down into the base of the wall will flow over the throughs and run away.

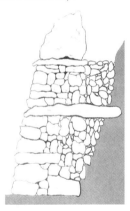

Retaining walls: single skin (left) and double skin (right)

Where drainage holes are necessary, these should be incorporated over the throughstones

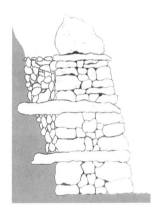

One of the difficulties when building retaining walls is that all work on the back face has to be carried out 'overhand', i.e. from the front. Once the wall is at waist height, if the waller brings the front face up by a couple of courses and then starts on the back wall there is a tendency to lean on the front when placing stones at the back. You may find that building the back wall one course higher <u>before</u> bringing up the front makes wedging easier and prevents the front stones from being pushed in. Do not go beyond one course, however, as this would make correct packing of the wall very difficult.

BUILDING FEATURES

The craft of dry stone walling has developed far beyond the provision of stock proof boundaries. The normal agricultural features that fulfilled specific functions out of necessity (wallheads, stiles and lunkies) have developed into decorative and artistic walling and this section describes the basic principles involved in building many of these features.

It is always a good thing to get a feel for what is needed before attempting to build a complex feature: it may be advisable to seek advice or to employ a professional waller. Details for contacting professional wallers can be obtained from the Association. (See Appendix 1)

Any project should be carefully planned. Stone is heavy and expensive, both to purchase and to transport. Access to your site is extremely important and if stone is to be tipped, protection of your drive must be considered. If it is necessary to deposit material on the public highway, you must first check regulations with your local authority.

It is always easier to move stone down a slope than up, but often, if features are required in an upward-sloping rear garden, access is at the lowest point. In this case you need to schedule plenty of time to move the stone to your walling site.

Remember that for each square metre of wall a tonne or more of stone will be needed. This may have to be barrowed to the walling site and if you are the landowner and are employing a skilled craftsman to build the feature it may be most cost-effective to do the barrowing yourself.

Sometimes, a feature built close to the house reduces access to the rest of the garden and this may make it harder for later work to be carried out: careful planning should prevent difficulties.

STEPS

There are two approaches to the building of steps. The first, and possibly the more artistic, makes best use of the stone you have available, and often results in smaller, less regular steps. The second demands the sourcing and obtaining of the ideal stone for each part. Both methods have their place and the basic construction principles remain the same.

If you are fortunate enough to have sufficient large, flat stones that are thick enough so that each has the correct dimensions as both the riser and the tread, then little additional building is needed; but if stones are thinner and do not create a step with a 20-25cm rise, you should proceed as follows.

Assuming that the steps are to provide access to higher ground, then there will be a retaining wall or earth bank to break into. The gap removed must be somewhat larger than the dimensions of the stone used plus backfilling. When digging out, all spoil should be moved well to the side of the working area to allow easier manoeuvring of heavy stones.

If you are using large, heavy stone flags of at least 7.5cm, then before setting each you need to build a level, low single face wall to ensure that the total rise is 20-25cm when the flag is in position.

Carefully pack behind this wall with stone, ramming it well down into the subsoil until the level reaches the top of the wall. Experience indicates that there seems to be more settling at the rear of the tread so, if anything, this should be fractionally higher.

Now lay your slab so that it projects over the edge of the front riser wall by 2cm (this will ensure that water drops clear of the riser). Next build your wall on both sides of the slab so that the weight holds it firmly in place.

In building your next step, ensure that the usable tread from the front edge to the back is over 25cm to allow even the largest boot to fit comfortably on to the step. Make a line here and build another low riser wall in the same way as for the first step, although at this point it should be set on the slab so that it applies weight to the rear of it. Building with a very slight slope of around 2cm down to the front edge helps to ensure that as the slab settles it does not drop too low at the back. This slight slope will also prevent water lying on the step: constant dampness provides a happy home for algae, which would make the surface slippery.

Having repeated this pattern until you reach the top step, finish off with the final slab (see opposite) set just above the ground level. This too will settle over a few months of use to its finished level.

If you are using very large, thick stones to form the steps, you may not need the low walls as risers, but remember the stones will be exceptionally heavy and probably beyond the lifting capability of one person. These stones often need resetting several times until they sit to your satisfaction and you risk injury if you try to lift them unaided: seek help for this part of the job. The same principles of tying in the edges of the stone with the side walls apply, as does the need to seat a higher step on the back edge of the previous one.

When thick stones are available they can be successfully used in steps but ensure help is available for lifting and positioning

STEP-STILES

Occasionally there is a need to provide a way through or over a freestanding wall, perhaps where a footpath crosses it, or simply to provide access to the field or garden beyond while preventing the entry of livestock. In this case a wide gap cannot be created and in some cases even a small gap will allow lambs through. To prevent this, a variety of step-stiles have been developed.

Although there are two basic types - a step-over stile allowing the person to climb over the wall with ease, and a step-through stile involving a tapering gap in the wall – you will see variations and combinations of the two where the waller has used ingenuity and the stone that he has to best advantage.

The step-over stile is the most likely to be found in areas where there are sufficient very long, flattish stones of suitable thickness and strength, and where fields are normally used for sheep. To build this type of stile you ideally need three or more very long stones, 120-130cm in length, or half-a-dozen at 80-100cm. These need to be thick enough to bear the weight of any walker.

Using the longer stones (the better option), you raise your double wall to a height at which, when your longest stone is laid centrally across the wall, the top of the stone will be approximately 30cm above ground. This stone should project equally on each side of the wall by about 30cm and should have a flat, not convex, top surface on which the walker can place one foot securely.

The wall is raised across this large stone, and the next step-stone is put in place. Its front edge should be immediately above, or very slightly overlapping, the rear edge of the step-stone below it, so that walkers will not lose their footing and slip between the two steps.

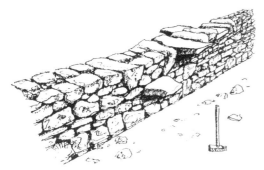

With shorter stones for creating steps, the stones protrude one side only and walkers cross on the diagonal

If you are using shorter stones, and more of them, then as in the diagram, they only project on one side of the wall; this means there is no weight on the other side to counterbalance the projecting section of stone or the weight of the person using the stile. With shorter stones it is usual for the stile to be built so that walkers cross at the diagonal, without having to turn back on themselves as they do with double-width step-stones.

The last step should not be placed too near the top of the wall, because like the others it needs as much weight of stone above it as possible to stop it from rocking and displacing the copestones.

This type of stile can be finished with a large, heavy flagstone instead of copestones on top of the wall. This does not project on either side, and has the advantage of showing walkers from a distance where the next stile is as it breaks the continuity of the top line of the wall.

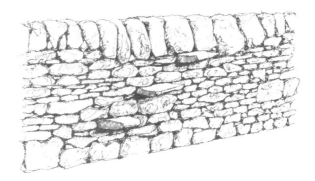

Very long stones protrude on both faces of the wall, the walker turns when crossing.
Note the heavy copes securing the top step.

SQUEEZE STILES

Squeeze stiles – where walkers squeeze through a gap in the wall - occur widely throughout the British Isles. The aim is to provide a tapering gap, formed by two cheekends or wallheads, which is large enough for a person's body to squeeze through but too narrow as it reaches the bottom for livestock to do the same. These squeeze gaps are an ideal solution in cattle country, but sheep and lambs may find them no problem if they wish to make a break for freedom.

Various methods have been developed to modify this simple structure of wallheads to make it more difficult for sheep and lambs to use.

Two of these are illustrated. In the first case the wall is built to approximately throughstone height and the squeeze gap is constructed above it. From a lamb's point of view the wall looks impenetrable, and by the time it is big enough to scramble up on to the step, it will probably be too fat to squeeze through the gap.

In the second case, where local stone supplies allow, the gap is crossed with an upright flagstone set into the two opposing wallheads. The walker steps on to the flat throughstone, and then steps over the tightly held upright flag.

As in all cases where a wall coping is breached for access, the adjacent copestones must be large and have a solid, square base. Heavily laden walkers always grasp these end copestones to steady themselves as they cross the wall.

This problem may be overcome if you have very long stones available, at least 45cm longer than the height of the wall. The first long stone is bedded on end in a hole dug tight to the first wallhead, leaned against it and well rammed in. The second wallhead is built at the correct distance from the first large stone, allowing room for the second upright stone which is then dug in to mirror the first. Old stone gateposts (stoops) that have broken off at, or just below, ground level are ideal for this purpose. The top of the long stones rather than the end copestone is now the lever used by the walkers.

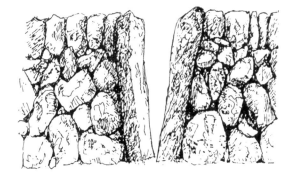

Moving, placing, securing and packing these stoops is unquestionably a two-man job unless mechanical handling is available.

If a flat stone or flag can be found to set in the ground between the sides of a squeeze stile it will help prevent erosion of the path at that point. Similarly, a large flat stone can be placed at ground level on step-stiles.

LUNKY, HOGG OR CRIPPLE HOLES

These features are often found in upland areas where sheep have traditionally been kept. They are openings built into the lower part of the wall, which allow sheep or lambs to pass through without the farmer needing to come and open gates.

Technically, lunky holes consist of two low wallheads crossed by a single large flag or by two touching lintel stones; the wall above is completed in the normal way. These holes often have an adjacent step-stile to allow the shepherd to cross the wall. Lunkies may be closed with a boulder or slab when not in use.

A smaller sized lunky may also be built to allow lambs through and retain the ewes: this is a way of enabling lambs to graze fresh, young grass untainted with worm eggs dropped from the mother. Other small gaps, sometimes called smoots, allow rabbits and hares free movement: in earlier times such mammals were an important source of food and the small smoots could be netted to catch any animals chased into them.

Lunky hole in a Galloway Dyke

Wherever lunkies or smoots are constructed it is a good idea to pave the base with a slab, or better still to run the foundation course completely across the gap beneath it. This prevents erosion of the soil inside the lunky: such erosion would cause a dip, which would hold water. A paved base also reduces the likelihood of the wallheads settling or slipping sideways, and thus increases the life of the lunky considerably.

WATERPENS, WATERGATES OR WATERSMOOTS

Sometimes it is necessary to carry a wall across a small watercourse. Such work is always best undertaken – perhaps obviously - during the driest possible conditions and even then the water may need to be diverted to enable the base of any piers or pillars to be constructed.

A series of lunky holes will continue a wall across a small watercourse

Begin by digging in good solid stones well below the base of the stream or ditch. Large slabs should then be used to build upon these, with as few gaps as possible for the water to work on. In some areas plenty of clay is available, and this can be puddled into the middle of the pillar or pier up to the normal level of the water, making the pier impervious. Building pillars in this way can also enable the wall to be extended across a wide, shallow stream using a series of lintels to support it, like an aqueduct. When a wall is to cross a small ditch, you can just use a simple lunky.

In building features such as these, always make allowance for the increased volume of water during times of heavy rainfall. If the gaps are not sufficiently large to accommodate an unrestricted flow of water, a build-up of pressure will occur and the wall will be damaged.

Simple bridges (as opposite) can be constructed using similar principles to those described above; in every case for safety the lintels should be set well on to the piers supporting each end.

CURVES

Curved stone walls add a different dimension to the craft of walling. They can reduce the formality of a garden, but are also sometimes needed in fieldwork when taking a straight wall around a tree, or when building sheep pens and similar features.

Constructing a curve using walling frames can be very difficult and a combination of good judgement and some pegs or iron bars will be very useful.

The setting out for a curve, whether it is free standing or retaining, should be approached with care. You need to mark out the base with as many pegs as possible, moving and adjusting them until you get a smooth curve. This will provide the outside edge of your foundation trench. Measure in from each one of these pegs – do not skimp at this stage - and set out your line of inner pegs.

The easiest way to provide yourself with a guide to the batter for a curve is to replace the pegs with thick canes or metal bars as soon as your foundations are in place. A smoothly rising curve can also be achieved by using a string attached to a metal rod hammered into the ground at the centre of the incomplete circle of which the curve forms a part. The string can be shortened as the wall rises, to check that the outer batter is correct. A second string can be used to check the curvature of the inside: if the inner face is to be battered, the string needs to be lengthened as the wall rises.

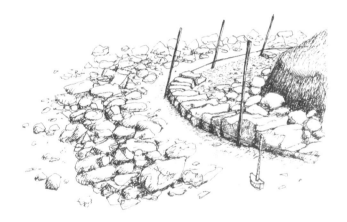

Curved wall showing metal bars in place to determine batter

It is possible to check the evenness of the outside curve by eye as long as you get close to the wall. For a smooth result, stones that are short in length (along the wall) and slightly wedge-shaped should be chosen. These can be set with very small gaps, stone to stone, whereas square or oblong stones touch at their back edge and leave large gaps at the front. This is where careful use of the hammer on the internal edges of the stone can tighten the work up considerably.

Your canes or bars provide a guide to batter, your eye determines the evenness of the curve. It is possible to use bars as a guide to forming the inside face, but sighting around an inside curve is just about impossible. You can try to check with hand and eye by looking down from above, but do not do this by leaning on the wall. Any pressure against the outside face may cause a distortion in the curve, particularly in the upper courses.

Should you be building a wall with a number of curves in it you will find that laying out the shape is easiest if you form the curves from thick rope or hosepipe, and measure them from a straight baseline.

ARCHES

Dry stone arches demand careful sorting and preparation of stone, and the creation of a special template, before construction work begins.

Any arch will attempt to transfer forces sideways as the weight of the stone above pushes downwards. There needs to be a sufficiently solid section of wall already built on each side of the gap over which the arch is to be built to withstand this sideways pressure.

Solid wall with upright timber supports in place, note wedges at ground level which can be more easily removed at end of work, and semicircular template in position ready to build arch similar to that opposite

Various materials have been used for arch templates, from car tyres to redundant barrels. If the template is to stay in position for some time, it is worthwhile constructing it of plywood, or slatted timber, to the dimensions and shape required; such a template could be reused.

Two pieces of 15mm plywood, shaped as required and joined by 75mm x 25mm slats, are all that is needed. These can be raised on shortened building planks to make a walk-through arch 2m high. The base of each of the planks is wedged up so that it lies vertically against the wallheads that form the sides of the arch.

Smaller arches need less in the form of a template; other examples are show in the diagrams. Again, if you use wedges beneath the template these can be removed when construction is completed to allow the form – not the stones, naturally – to drop out.

The stones for arch construction need to be regular and, if possible, slightly tapering. Ideally they should be long enough to be cut to the full width of the wall. If possible, stones should be selected and matched so that they look well balanced on both sides of the central stone, or keystone, in the arch.

Once the template is in place, you can begin construction of the curved arch either from ground level or from the top of a vertical wallhead. Wedge each stone securely as you place it at the correct angle. The centre line of the stone should run along the radius of the imaginary circle of which your arch forms a part.

Work equally upwards, stepping back to check from both sides that you are working evenly. Where flat stones are used, the gaps at the top will need to be filled with tapering wedges.

Small keystone arch in freestanding wall with plywood template awaiting removal

Finally, place the keystone and wedge it if necessary, and then complete the wall over the top of the arch. As long as the stones in the wall have been laid tightly up to the ones which form the arch there will be no sideways movement, and once the template is removed, downward pressure will lock the arch stones tightly together. Where the arch stones taper slightly there may be no need for wedges between them.

Finally, remove the wedges from below the template: this will give sufficient room to slide it out without pulling on any stones.

A word of warning: you should build a number of low arches to get the feel of the technique before attempting a walk-through one. Full-sized arches need to be constructed while standing on some form of scaffolding so that you are above the arch stones and can see where any wedges are needed. Walk-through arches also need to be built into a high wall, with the wall continuing above the arch, for weight to provide stability.

When building corbelled arches, weight transfer is via the ends of the stones that reach back into the wall. The stones above should trap at least half, and preferably more, of each stone in the archway. If it is possible to find a long stone to stretch right across the top of the arch (as opposite), then this will add stability to the structure.

PILLARS

Whether building round or square pillars, you need to allow plenty of time and to have a good choice of stone. Pillars can be used to finish a wall (in which case they are either an upward extension of the wall top, or are built larger than the end of the wall) or they may be a combination of the two. In some cases, pillars need to be built free standing as part of a feature, such as a sundial or bird table.

When building a square pillar a good supply of long, regular stones with right-angled corners is essential. Corners can be made using a hammer, but length is perhaps more important since long stones tie the faces of the pillar together and without them it may be weak and unstable.

The corners of the square pillar are each built as described in the section on wall corners. Each course should be checked for width and across the diagonal. Where the pillar is not too wide, a template can be made out of wire or wood and used to check the square.

Round pillars have to be built as continuous, tight curves and need plenty of small, wedge-shaped stones to ensure a tight fit at the face. It is also a good idea regularly to insert longer stones that reach well into the centre like spokes in a wheel: these act like throughstones. It is unlikely that you will be able to use true throughstones, but do so if possible. Again, a wire or wooden template in the form of a hoop can be used. Round pillars and other circular features can be built using a metal rod driven into the ground at the centre point, and a string of the correct length tied with a loop around the rod can be used to provide the measure of the radius as each course is laid.

Whether building square or round pillars, it is essential that the centre be well packed. A great deal of small hearting will be needed and the inner edges of the face stones need to be well wedged.

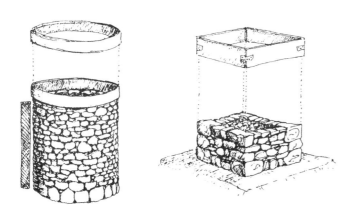

Round and square pillars under construction using basic shapes for templates

When any pillar is finished, it needs topping off with a flat flag or heavy copestone. If it is left open, the upper courses will begin to splay out and the pillar will soon deteriorate. An appealing finish may be achieved by topping with a large flag, cut to fit, with an interestingly shaped stone or even a sculpture placed centrally on the flat surface, adding weight like the cope on a finished wall. Once again, this is a case where two people must be involved in the lifting as the large top stone needs to be placed carefully and gently on top of the pillar. Take care that every stone in the final course of the pillar is firmly held in place by the top stone.

SHOOTING BUTTS

It is rare nowadays for new shooting butts to be built as few new grouse moors are being opened. However, this type of structure is becoming popular for seating or picnic shelters in parks and amenity areas.

Most work on shooting butts is confined to repair, and the original design and stonework should be followed. In the case of a new butt, it needs to be large enough to accommodate two people with ease, and if possible it could have built-in ledges and nooks for ammunition and food. In order to hide the gun and loader from the birds, shooting butts are recessed into the ground and location is usually decided by the gamekeepers or ghillies in order to give the best line of sight, or to facilitate a line of guns.

Circular butts are the norm, so the techniques used are as described in the section on curved walls. Butts are usually built with an entrance on the side away from the direction in which shooting takes place, and the entrance is usually some form of squeeze stile to keep out livestock.

The height of the topped wall should be such that an average person can easily sight his gun over the wall while not being seen by the birds. A shooting butt is frequently topped off with two layers of thick turf, the first laid grass side down, the upper layer with grass side uppermost. Once the grass grows, it will break the static line of the top of the butt.

Shooting butt of traditional circular design, built with single wall or boulder dyke coped with turf to reduce risk of damage to gun barrels.

REGIONAL VARIATION IN FIELD WALLS

COTSWOLD WALLS

The Cotswold style of building is similar to that used on a normal doubled wall, but with a number of distinct characteristics which have developed to make best use of and increase the life of the county's local oolitic limestone.

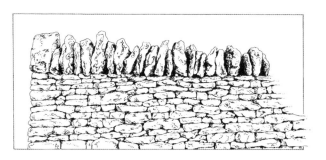

Cotswold walls are built on footings set in a very shallow trench with a base width of 60cm. Traditional field walls are no more than one metre high, including the cope, and may be built without throughstones although three-quarter throughs may be used. These walls are built with almost no batter, the top width being approximately three-quarters that of the base.

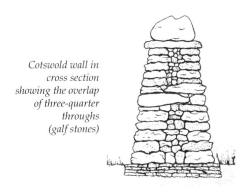

Cotswold wall in cross section showing the overlap of three-quarter throughs (galf stones)

The major difference is in the building of the body of the wall. Stones here are laid with a slight downward slope to the outside (watershot). This is to ensure that water does not run into the wall and lodge there. Oolitic limestone is extremely susceptible to chemical weathering and if it lies wet it blows or flakes and its life is shortened.

Stones are often trace walled (laid with the length along rather than into the wall) in order to make use of the best faces. This can cause poor binding and a weak wall.

The Cotswold waller makes great use of his hammer on newly quarried stone. This is quite soft, and he is able to take great pride in producing a dressed, even face to a new wall. Carefully dressed wallheads are built using beautifully dressed corners (quoins) and the walls are often topped off with a mortar band in which are bedded upright, rough top stones known as combers.

SINGLE WALLS AND BOULDER DYKES

Single walls are largely confined to the northern areas of the UK where igneous rocks such as granite are to be found. They are built using massive, often rough boulders which are raised in a single row and wedged into position. These rocks are extremely hard and durable; they rarely break down into sizes which are small enough to provide suitable stone for double-faced walls.

Large stones such as these are used, often by a pair of wallers, to build single walls or boulder dykes. This is a type of wall where familiarity with the stone is vital: a good eye for picking the correct stone is necessary as each one is very heavy.

Set a single line to keep the wall straight, a little higher than the size of the stones to be used in the first course. It is unlikely that the stone will all be of a size to enable straight edges to be achieved, but each stone is manoeuvred into position with care and is then wedged tight. The largest stones should be used as foundations and dug into the ground with well-secured stones forming the wallhead. Stones should be well pinned at the base to prevent any movement. Try to ensure that these base stones are laid so that they do not sit with points upwards as this would make the securing of subsequent stones more difficult.

When you are satisfied that your first course is well set, raise the string and begin the second course. If the stones are large it helps to set up a plank as a ramp, and roll the stones up into position. The second course is jammed between the stones below, and it will probably take some pushing and pulling until each one drops nice and tightly into position. Where there is a pointed rock in the course below, you may have to bridge it. Again, pin and wedge stones if necessary. As the wall gets higher the stones should be smaller. Raise your line to the final level, and top off the wall.

Where possible, stones placed on higher levels should be set so that they lock into the gaps in the lower stones, breaking the joints. Handling these stones is not for the beginner and can often only be achieved with the aid of help, plus wooden ramps and crowbars. It is still important to try to cover each joint in walls of this type, despite the size of the stone.

The final wall will measure about 25cm wide at the top, where the aim is to finish with copes to leave a level top at about 1.5m high.

A method is illustrated above of careful use of irregular stone to cover joints while leaving a good bearing surface for the next stone.

GALLOWAY DYKES

The Galloway dyke is a special type of construction most commonly found in the south west of Scotland. It can be considered intermediate between double and single walls, as it makes best use of the flatter, smaller stone and the rounded glacial boulders that are both found in that area. The wallers of the past would have developed this method to use stone that was available at that time and near at hand.

Dykes can be built to accommodate large boulders immovably set in the ground; sometimes such boulders are so wide that they protrude from the face of the dyke.

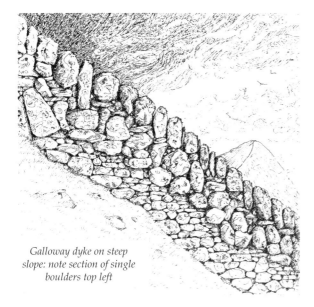

The wall is built as a normal double wall up to throughstone height with the smaller stone. The throughstones must reach right across the double and sometimes protrude beyond both faces. The largest boulders are then used to raise the structure as a single wall above the level of the throughstones. Once again, this is work to be carried out by dykers working in pairs as raising boulders high has safety implications.

The boulders are locked together by their own weight. Pins and wedges are sometimes used. These boulders (seconders) may be all that is needed to raise the wall to the full height but if not, a further row of boulders is added as before, sitting in the recesses of the row below.

Galloway dyke on steep slope: note section of single boulders top left

At this stage the copestones are ready for fitting. A line is set to the finished height, normally at 1.5m which is a little higher than the traditional double dyke. Two copestones are placed on the wall approximately 10 metres apart, and a line tied tightly to give a top level. The copestones are fixed as before and pinned with wedges of stone. The finished appearance of this type of dyke is rugged but it is designed as an agricultural dyke to enclose fields. It is said that sheep do not attempt to scramble over these as the small gaps between the boulders make them look unsafe!

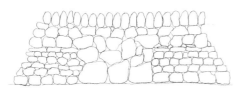

Many Galloway dykes are constructed with sections of single boulder dyke interspersed with sections of double topped with single

Many dykers from the region believe that the true Galloway dyke was built with alternating sections as in the diagram above interspersed with sections built as single dyke. This may have been developed because a good deal of larger stone was available, or simply because it was thought to produce a stronger wall.

FLAG FENCES

Flag fences can sometimes be found in areas where beds of layered sandstone have been quarried, for example Caithness or some parts of the Pennines, or where metamorphic slates are found as in Cumbria or North Wales. These flags are set upright in a slit trench with about one third of their length buried in the ground.

There is variation in how they are fitted together. Caithness flags are often overlapped, Cumbria flags are often worked at the edges so that they fit together with halving joints, and the Pennine ones are simply butt jointed with even more depth buried in the ground for stability (see below). In North Wales, narrow lengths of slate can be seen stabilised by horizontal wires running the length of the wall and twisted between each upright.

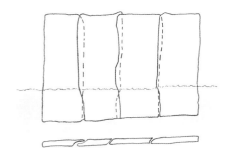

Cumbrian or Lakeland style (left) showing the 'interwoven' joints.
Pennine (right) butted up where the flags meet

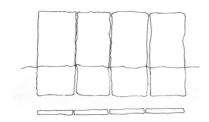

STONE HEDGES AND STONE-FACED EARTH BANKS

These are to be found mainly in the western areas of the British Isles. They are known as hedges in Cornwall, banks in Devon and clawdd or cloddiau in Wales.

There is a variety of styles in these walls that can be seen varying from parish to parish, but all involve construction using a core of subsoil or similar material. A typical free-standing Cornish hedge stands about 1.5 metres high, with a similar base width, though these hedges can reach three metres in some areas. They are built on a wide base approximately equal to the height, and narrow to half that width at the top.

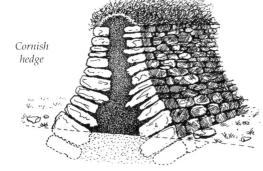

Cornish hedge

© TF Wragg

Landscape: dry stone walls are an important part of the landscape, particularly in upland regions where they can become a relevant feature for tourists, as in Derbyshire above.

Field patterns can be used to determine the period in which a field boundary was created.

The stone makes a great difference in the appearance
of dry stone walls, but many are constructed in a
similar manner: the Association's branches created
the Millennium Wall at the National Stone Centre
(Wirksworth, Derbyshire) to bring onto a single site
vernacular field walls from various parts of Britain.

*Clockwise from top right:
plinth of Carboniferous
limestone and sandstone;
Cumbrian Borrowdale
volcanic green slate;
Lancashire Haslingden flags
(Carboniferous Millstone
Grit); Derbyshire's
combination to show the
White and Dark Peak with
Carboniferous limestone and
Gritstone.*

*Double walls
(top)
Northumbria
displaying a step
stile in Ganister
sandstone;
(below left)
South East
Scotland dyke of
Dolerite or
Whinstone;
(below right)
section of South
Wales wall built
with Blue
Pennant
(gritstone)*

The Isle of Skye double dyke of basalt with a turf cope

Cheshire wall of Milnrow sandstone with early covering of lichen

Some exhibits in the Millennium Wall are distinctively regional

South West Scotland's Galloway dyke of glacial erratic granite boulders

(below left) A single dyke from Sutherland of welded quartzite

(below right) A Cumbrian slab wall in Brathay blue slate

Walls are important as field boundaries

Rebuilt farm wall in north Wales forms a significant landscape feature

Galloway dyke – this example built without sections of single walling

This Cumbrian wall in Langdale comes to a stream which has fluctuating water levels: note the use of timber set into cheekend to support a wire gate which allows water to flow in spate, but retains stock.

Attractive wall sympathetic to the landscape and the slight incline

Walls come in many shapes and sizes: some have added 'extras'

Boundary marker in Derbyshire wall
(© TF Wragg)

Retaining wall carrying old road with culvert: perhaps a suitable topic for a restoration project.
(© S Huguet)

Unusual Cumbrian combination of arched watersmoot with slate grid to trap debris in stream © Ian Brodie /FLD

Deer wall in south west Scotland with mortared cope

Bottom l-r:
Large boulders in base of wall

Single dyke with stones laid vertically

**Walls provide valuable
habitats for wildlife**

*A selection
of mosses
and lichen
on dry
stone walls*

*Above: Cornish hedge awash
with wild flowers*

*Top right: a damp spot beside
a Yorkshire Dales wall*

*Right: ivy conceals a nesting
blackbird*

Dry stone walls are the gardeners delight

Retaining walls with trailing plants: a good contrast of texture and colour

High walls for privacy or shelter, low ones to create varying levels and focal points within the garden

Above left: Dumfries - colourful garden corner enhanced by low dry stone retaining wall

Above right: Caithness slate wall between field and driveway providing an additional narrow raised flowerbed

Right: Cumbria - a carefully constructed niche for a bee skep, complete with skep and traditional equipment

Dry stone walling techniques are used in special commissions and works of art

Blackhouse on Harris, awarded DSWA's first ever Pinnacle Award

Below left: grotto in a convent garden

Right: Shibden Hall pillar displaying skills of dry stone walling and masonry

Right: The Royal Jubilee cipher created at Chatsworth for the Duke & Duchess of Devonshire to celebrate the golden jubilee of HM Queen Elizabeth II
© Bridget Flemming

The DSWA Pinnacle Award commends innovative and exceptional projects: below is part of an award winning project in Hertfordshire.

Intricately constructed sphere is a fountain. It formed part of an award-winning garden exhibit at the major RHS show in Cheshire: stone and water in harmony

Walls as they should not be built

This book would be incomplete without examples of work which a few individuals have called dry stone walling.

Having read the text can you now list the faults?

Round end in level-bedded sandstone

Wallhead: lack of batter and possibly held upright by its cemented cope.

Retaining wall, again in level-bedded stone: the road surface rises slightly to the left

Work in angular random stone: compare to that exhibited page 51, bottom left.

The foundation stones (grounders) are laid in a shallow trench and slant gently downwards towards the centre at a similar angle to that of the blade of a traditional Cornish shovel to its shaft (30-35 degrees). Although different styles of laying subsequent courses are to be found, with some placing stones vertically and others horizontally, in all cases joints are covered and the stones graded in size using the larger ones towards the base. As each course is laid, it is backfilled with damp, granular or shale-like subsoil (known as rab, growan, shillet). This is well compacted before moving on to the next course.

Traditionally, the wall is built with a concave batter, a characteristic which is found in other coastal parts of the country where penetrating frosts are less likely. It finishes with further fill in a domed profile to allow for settling, and is often covered with turf that overlaps the top course.

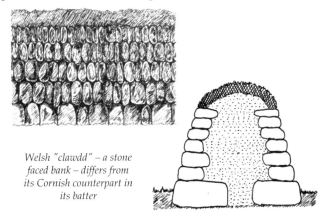

Welsh "clawdd" – a stone faced bank – differs from its Cornish counterpart in its batter

The Welsh equivalent to the Cornish hedge is the clawdd (the plural is cloddiau – literally "walls", though colloquially taken to be stone faced banks). These differ from the Cornish hedge largely in their batter, and in the fact that the foundations are laid level. All joints are covered, or in the case of vertically laid stonework, the next course of stones is set so that they drive down into the wedge left between the stones of the layer below. The core of subsoil or rubble and subsoil mix of the clawdd is topped with turf.

TURF TOPS

The most popular method of topping off with turf is to use a double layer. This is laid on the wall with the first layer grass downwards: it will in time rot and feed the second layer, which is laid grass up. The divots should be laid with the joints of the two layers overlapping so that, should the top dry out, cracks are less likely to develop the whole way through. This type of top is best used in areas where there is sufficient regular rainfall to keep it well watered.

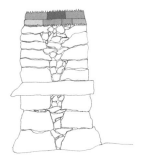

MORTARED COPES

There are two main reasons for using mortar on wall tops.

a)   In the Cotswolds, large stones are rare and the material is soft. Top stones are sometimes omitted and the whole of the cope is replaced with a slightly domed layer of mortar.

b)   There are cases, particularly alongside roads, where to prevent theft or vandalism copestones are secured with a mortar band along the top of the wall and with pads of mortar between them. This however brings its own problems: as the subsoil compacts and the wall settles a little lower the top courses may break away from the more firmly held line of copes above. This removes pressure from the stones in this area of the wall and they begin to sag outwards and downwards. Finally, the wall is left with a gap above the top courses which is bridged by the mortared copes. This is a dangerous situation that renders the whole of that section of wall unstable.

IMPROVING YOUR TECHNIQUE & SPEED

In striving to become a better waller, anyone can learn by watching and talking to others. This section offers tips and suggestions that have been gathered from skilled craftsmen and women around Britain.

1.   When stripping down and laying out stone for a rebuild, do not assume that where a stone was previously placed is its ideal position. The occasional copestone, for example, might have been used in the lower area of the wall.

2.   Before building, set up your line of copestones on end. You can see their individual heights this way and if you need a shorter or taller one, it can easily be spotted.

3.   Any wedges to be used for securing the copes can easily be trodden into the ground and lost. When stripping down, place them in a pile near your copestones, and then move them close to the wall when you are ready to begin putting your copes on.

4.   Many wallers find that they miss good stone which should be in the lower part of the wall because it is buried by other stone in a big general pile. It is always good practice to give yourself as much working space as possible. This is especially important if you are building a well-coursed wall: you need to lay the stone out on edge with the face upwards. A little time spent doing this is rapidly regained as you select the correct thickness of stone much more quickly. The extra space allows you to place stones of similar thickness together. Walls built in level-bedded stone of similar thickness are unforgiving if a thicker stone is out of place amongst them.

5.   Try to use all large stones in the lower part of the wall. If placed above the throughstones they look out of place; they may also project too far into the wall, leaving little space for stone on the other face. They also affect the quality of finish as they rarely taper to fit well with the batter.

6.   Do not make your foundation course too narrow if building on soft ground. The weight of the wall will cause less settlement if the foundation is wider.

Scarcement constructed below ground to spread weight of wall

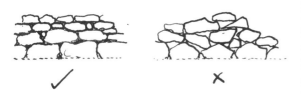

7.   When building a coursed wall, try to keep all building true to the horizontal. Stone is less likely to slip if laid this way. It is unlikely that a small deviation will cause problems - in fact, many walls built on slightly rising ground follow the slope - but once the angle gets over ten degrees, it is advisable to lay the courses horizontally.

8.   Few wallers can build a stretch of really straight wall without the use of lines. There may be those who feel they can, but it is unwise to work without when you are aiming for quality.

9.   When building the faces of the wall, try to ensure the stone is level from outside to inside. The only area where this rule is not applied is when building field and garden walls with stone that is likely to be attacked or softened by weak acid, as is the case with the oolitic limestone in the Cotswolds which is often laid watershot. Building with the tails of the stones dipping down into the middle of the wall is never good practice.

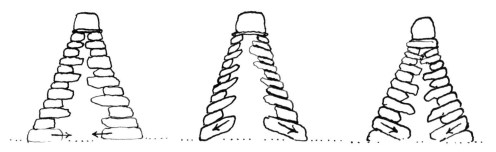

Cross-sections to show three ways of laying stone (l-r)
Level as most commonly occurs
Tilted outwards (exaggerated in diagram)
Inwards tilt – not recommended in normal conditions

10. When rebuilding a wall you can tell which way the stones were originally laid as exposure to the atmosphere results in algae and lichen growth on the outside face of stones. Do not blindly put stones back the way they were previously placed. Sometimes wallers cut corners and laid long, narrow stones with their length along the wall (this is known as trace walling) to achieve greater speed. This practice results in more hearting than strength to that face of the wall, and weakens it. The occasional trace walled stone does little harm as long as it is balanced by long stones into the wall on the other side and is well weighted from above.

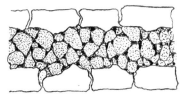

Trace walling viewed from above

11. When placing stones, your fingers become a good guide to how well the stones sit. If you feel for gaps below the stones, you soon become accustomed to the size and shape of pins needed to support them properly. Your fingers are also a useful guide to developing the batter on the wall: if you step each course back half a finger's width or more as appropriate, you will find the wall narrows by the correct amount as it rises.

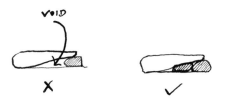

12. Building stones should be well supported by wedges from the back edge and underneath the stone to reduce the risk of their snapping as a result of pressure from above. Never build several courses up on one side and then start on the other: it is impossible to pack or pin correctly. This would be a failure point in DSWA certification tests.

13. When packing the wall with hearting, start by placing the largest pieces, then pack around them with smaller and smaller material. This reduces the likelihood of voids being left. Large pieces of hearting should be used in the lower half of the wall, where they are most useful.

14. It is much easier to see if faults are developing in your work if you step back from the wall. Looking from a few metres away shows up potential problems such as vertical joints. It is also important to look along the line of the wall regularly to detect any deviation from the straight line that you are trying to achieve.

15. It is easy when coursing material that is regular in length to develop a fault where each stone overlaps a similar one on the course below by a small amount. When you step back from the wall this shows up as an ugly diagonal like a flight of steps - a running joint. You can avoid this by using short stones at appropriate intervals to break up the regular placing of the stones.

16. If you work with a build up of stone and soil close to the wall, making the ground seem to slope a little towards the wall, hollows or bows in the wall face may well develop at these points. This is because you are tilted forward slightly, often pushing against the outside face of the stonework as you place stones on the wall, and the face of the wall can move slightly inwards.

Do not allow soil and debris to build up in working area, your knees will constantly push into the wall as you work

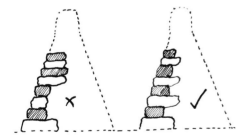

17. Never use stones with little depth into the centre in the lower sections of the wall if you can possibly avoid it. Where it becomes unavoidable, for example to accommodate a stone which runs deeply in from the other face, reverse this situation on the next course so the narrow one is covered by a wider one. Never cover a narrow stone with a similar one as this will seriously weaken the face of the wall at that point.

18. When working with very thin stone, your progress will be slow if you seek out and collect just one stone at a time. Much better both for your body and your speed to stack four or five, more if you can, stones of the same thickness on your arm and take them to the wall. You can place, adjust and pin them with only one movement away from the wall and one bend of your back.

19. Little is achieved by forcing pins into the face of the wall. The effect may be to suggest that the wall has been built more tightly than it has, but this is only cosmetic. The forcing in of pins may raise stones so that they are less securely seated. Any small gaps must be filled with appropriately shaped stones that reach well back into the wall as you build. If the stone is a wedge shape it will be forced out as the wall tightens.

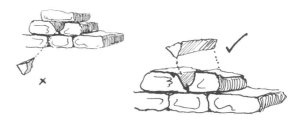

Never force pins into the face between stones: fill small gaps with appropriately shaped stones as you build

20. Once foundations are set, fill in any gap alongside the wall with excavated soil. This reduces the risk of twisted ankles or trapped feet in any remaining excavated trench.

USING NATURAL STONE IN THE GARDEN

Gardening is a most popular pastime in Britain, and millions enjoy planning, creating and planting their immediate surroundings. The use of dry stone work in the garden opens up infinite opportunities for creating the most interesting and unusual features. Dry stone also enables gardeners to solve problems such as less attractive views, lack of privacy or steep slopes while transforming the look of their plot.

Stone offers major benefits to the gardener. It is an ideal medium to use in landscaping for it is totally natural and will blend into any setting. It adds an extra dimension of height to a garden, giving support to climbing plants and a home to birds and other wildlife. Stone absorbs heat during the day and slowly releases it at night, so plants nearby enjoy a longer growing season and gain a certain protection from frost. This makes it possible for tender plants to be grown further north than would otherwise be possible; in fact the shelter that walls provide can be valuable on any exposed site and an adventurous gardener will be able to take full advantage of this.

In previous sections of this book you will find building techniques and tips on how to build features, but remember that there is no substitute for 'hands on' experience. If you intend to do some or all of the work yourself, it is strongly recommended that you attend one of the many short courses in dry stone walling held periodically around the country.

Wherever possible, you should use the stone that occurs naturally in your area unless you are intending to make a feature of a monolith or cluster of unusual rocks. The same applies when building a rockery: mixing stone types never works well.

PLANNING

Any form of construction work in the garden involves forethought and planning. Consideration should be given to your source of stone and its access for delivery (stone is heavy and needs to be stored close to its position of use). Wet weather deliveries may cause damage to the ground. Tipping of stone on roads or drives should be avoided and clarification sought from the local authority before tipping on any public road – however quiet it may be.

Where stone has to be tipped on drives or paths, thick sheets of plywood should be used to spread the weight and prevent surface damage. If the stone can be delivered to the highest point possible, much time and energy can be saved in its movement to the building site. In some situations, and especially on a new plot, firm access for moving stone may be a problem, while in an older garden access may be limited by the existing layout. Check plans to ensure that stone or machinery will not be damaging drains or underground services.

You may wish to employ a skilled craftsman and his advice should be sought in the planning stages to avoid later problems. Drainage, decorative features, new lawns, paths, flower borders and other allied work should be planned at the same time even if all the work is not going to be undertaken at an early stage. You should consider whether the garden is going to be formal, with symmetrical layout and areas devoted to particular planting themes, or informal with gentle curves and softened corners. Although certain features are more suited to larger gardens, smaller plots can equally be transformed by the use of stone. As a rule, more formal garden features should be placed nearer the house – particularly if the house is new or built of brick – and the wilder, more random features farther away. Points to consider and useful tips will be found in this section.

THE STONE

Stone imported from an area of different rock type looks out of place and invariably tends to detract from, rather than enhance, the landscape. However, many gardeners live in areas where there is not much usable stone, in which case a good rule of thumb is to buy it from the nearest available source. This material should blend in well and there is the bonus of reduced transport costs. The same principle applies to the style of building: if random stonework is the norm in your area, be wary of using coursed walling (walling in distinctive layers). The size of stone should be considered, particularly if you are doing the work yourself, because some regions utilise massive boulders that may be too much for you to manoeuvre safely.

MACHINERY

If you are embarking on an extensive garden project, the hiring of machinery such as a mini-digger, a powered wheelbarrow or even an excavator with driver may be cost-effective. Preparatory work for most garden projects however is frequently carried out by hand.

In the reshaping of an existing garden, plants should be lifted when dormant and replanted in their new positions, or heeled into a temporary bed to be replanted when the project is completed.

Try to use any excavated soil in another area of your garden, rather than hiring a skip to remove it. This is good conservation practice; and indeed the presence of surplus soil may open up the opportunity to construct a bank, a raised bed or rockery, or to level off a slope.

MAKING THE STONE WORK FOR YOU

With many modern houses the plots are either rectangular and flat, or steep and cut into a hillside. Occasionally, where they are built on reclaimed industrial land, the underlying soil and drainage are such that the only way to grow plants successfully is to create a raised bed with new topsoil.

Terracing with retaining walls has been the time-honoured method of taming steeply sloping sites, providing level areas in which shrubs and other plants can grow with a good root run in well-drained soil.

On flat, rectangular sites walls break the area up and add vertical planting surfaces. Walls may also be used around the boundaries but negotiation with neighbours and adherence to planning regulations has to be considered. If a boundary wall is not jointly owned, permission is required from your neighbour for access to his or her land during construction, and the waller will have to work overhand, building from one side only: this is slower and more expensive. In this situation, the wall will be totally on your ground.

Stone walls can be used to break up a large garden into different areas, creating new routes and vistas which may be concealed or revealed; they can also be used to create shapes and structures to add interest. Many of these features have been described in previous sections and where these are to be used, you should consider how and from where they are to be viewed.

If natural stone flags are available they can be used to create paths or terraces which combine beauty with low maintenance. When constructing such areas from scratch, the wise gardener will consider laying a weed-suppressing membrane below the compacted sand on which the slabs are bedded.

FINDING A CRAFTSMAN

If you are to employ someone for the work and do not already know a skilled craftsman, contact the Dry Stone Walling Association for their current list of certificated professionals. Entrusting your job to an unqualified person would be an expensive mistake.

Any form of garden landscaping is costly and walling is no exception. Dry stone work in gardens costs more than in farming situations, as there is more time involved, particularly in the selection and shaping of stone. It will help a great deal if you make sure your waller has a supply of clean stone in the right place at the right time. It may be stating the obvious, but do be certain that your craftsman understands your plans and your conception of the finished work!

WALLS AND PLANTS IN HARMONY

Many gardens have unsightly corners whose purpose is practical rather that beautiful, and dry stone walls can be used to screen these. They can be built in a variety of sizes, but where they are free standing, the ratio of top width to base should be kept at approximately 1:2.

A wall placed on the windward side of an herbaceous border can provide protection for tall-growing and spiky plants such as delphiniums, hollyhocks and lupins. Walls can also provide a useful habitat for climbing and trailing plants. Where these are self-clinging, like ivies, no additional support is necessary, but less self-sufficient plants like roses may need to be secured to the wall for best effect. If you wish to put plants actually into the wall, then this must be done sensibly without weakening the structure in any way (see later section on retaining walls).

Walls are a useful screen around vegetable gardens and, unlike hedges, have no roots to invade and feed on the nutrients of the growing area or compete with plants for water and light. Dry stone walls, unlike those using mortar and set on concrete footings, can act as a means of draining the ground via their foundations.

So dry stone walls in the garden have many advantages; but there are some drawbacks. Slugs, snails and other pests may move in and may attack vulnerable plants, though to some degree this is offset as their predators, such a shrews, spiders and slowworms, also find walls a pleasant habitat.

Dry stone walls around garden plots tend to dry out the soil around them. This may be a useful attribute in wet areas, but extra watering and mulching may be needed in dry periods if plants close to a wall are to grow well.

When you are setting plants close to walls, whether freestanding or retaining, you need to be aware of the damage that can be done as they grow. Walls can be disturbed both by the invasive nature of the roots, prising stones apart, and by vibration passed down into the soil in windy conditions. Trees and shrubs should not be planted too close to walls as it has been found that these can reduce the life of dry stone work considerably.

RAISED BEDS
Raised beds can provide a well-drained area in an otherwise wet garden, and can give the opportunity to use varying soil types or to create themed beds by growing different families of plants.

In limestone areas, a raised bed filled with a peat-based soil allows the growth of heathers, azaleas and rhododendrons without difficulty. In acidic areas, soils mixed with ground limestone may provide the perfect habitat for cowslips, thrift and other lime-lovers.

Narrow raised beds built to form planters dry out quickly and this may be the one occasion where the tails of the stones can be allowed to slope inwards and downwards to lead water into the plant roots and compensate for the drying properties of the wall.

Raised beds are particularly easy to manage for the disabled or those who find bending difficult. If combined with stone paths, they provide wheelchair access and if the low walls are topped with flat stones they give somewhere to sit while weeding. Raised beds need heavy top stones that will resist movement as you work on the bed.

The surface of raised beds can be finished with a thick layer of chippings and sand, which is particularly important where alpines are grown. These hate having their feet wet for any length of time. Alpine plants that are useful in this situation include aethionema, arabis, rockery penstemon e.g. pinifolius or rupicola, phlox douglasii, silene (campion) and rockery pinks.

ROCKERIES AND SCREE BEDS

Most horticulturists consider that the best rockeries are those modelled on natural outcrops. This means that very large stones are most suitable. Where these stones are placed on a slope or near any edge, two-thirds should be buried in the ground for stability and safety. The bedding planes on all rocks should tilt backwards at the same angle, creating the effect of rocks breaking out of the ground.

In nature, much of the rock is weathered into small pieces that, with erosion, gather on and at the base of the slope: these are scree beds. They are well drained and provide habitats for creeping or tussock-like alpines. In addition to those plants mentioned above, miniature bulbs, gentians, miniature geraniums and other alpines thrive here.

Rockeries and scree beds are, in fact, raised beds without the confines of walls and offer an ideal way of using up stony material excavated when building ponds or sunken gardens. One of the best ways to build a scree bed is to remove about 20 cm of soil from between the rock and fill the area with your waste broken stone. Then add 5cm of coarse sand, finishing off with about 3cm of a gritty compost. Plant your alpines into this, with the minimum of soil attached to the roots. Alpines need a free draining home and if contented they develop large root runs; they hate being damp during the winter and this gritty habitat provides the best conditions for their growth.

SUNKEN GARDENS

Changes of level in a garden add interest, and sometimes by lowering the level of an otherwise flat, featureless area it is possible to provide a sunken section and produce enough material for a raised bed or rock garden elsewhere. An already low area within a garden which might normally be hard to make the best of could also be developed into one of these striking and unusual features. Sunken gardens can be formal and regular in shape, with straight or curved walls: steps would be needed for access.

Being the lowest point of the garden, a sunken area is the collection point for water, and it may be a good idea to take advantage of this by creating a small pond or a formal water feature there. In any case, however, it is essential to install a means of guiding excess water to a drain or a stone soakaway.

There will be a great deal of excavation to be done, and a mini-digger hired for a day will save a lot of backache. The area excavated will need to be larger all round than the finished sunken space, to allow for proper filling behind the retaining walls.

Once the digging is done, building can begin. The sunken garden is simply a collection of retaining walls and corners, probably with a flight of steps for access. With thoughtful planning, a slightly higher wall could be built on the north side to reflect sun back into the sunken section and mitigate problems of shade to some degree.

Shade may in fact be quite a problem in a sunken garden. Grass does not do well in these conditions yet moss thrives. Camomile may be a better choice if you yearn for a lawn, but if the sunken area is to be well used it should be paved. If it is well drained and sunny, thyme and other low-growing herbs will flourish between the paving and smell delightful when trodden on. Some slabs may be set more widely apart to provide planting pockets. As with a patio, for easy maintenance, a membrane will minimise the need for weeding.

ARCHES

Arches may form an inviting opening to walk through to gain entry to a garden, or be constructed in walls within the garden. When smaller arches are set in walls, they may be of any size and shape, and may be open – allowing a glimpse of another section of the garden – or closed as a frame to set off a pot or trough filled with plants.

Closed arches are best built in retaining walls or low down in higher, freestanding walls. Where they are placed high up in a freestanding wall in exposed areas they are in danger of being damaged by the weather, as the wall will be weaker at this point.

NICHES

Niches are closed arches within a wall, support being created by the keystone method or with a lintel or corbels. They can be uses to enhance candles, lights or statues and can even be designed as closed shelves on which to lay out food and drink when barbecuing in the garden. Near the front door of your home, a niche can be a perfect place for milk bottles, a letter box or a good container of plants.

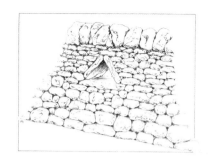

Where niches are built to hold skeps of bees (a very rare occurrence nowadays, though still to be seen in older gardens) they need to be built into a south-east facing wall, so that the colony of bees will be warmed by the morning sun and begin to forage early. The dimensions to enable a skep to fit comfortably are 45cm x 45cm x 40cm deep, and the base should be a minimum of 75 cm above the ground.

A selection of traditional bee boles showing use of the stone that was locally available

RETAINING WALLS

In some regions retaining walls are seen as high structures where deep cuts have been made through the hillside. In the garden, however, they can be used to provide decorative frontage supporting different soil levels and as the means of creating raised beds or sunken gardens. In these guises they may provide flat soil areas in which to grow many deeper-rooted plants as well as offering an ideal habitat for trailing vegetation.

Plants do need to be chosen carefully as the bed within the wall may become a small Sahara if it lies in full sun, or may offer cool damp conditions if in the shade.

If you wish to plant flowers directly into the wall, then this must be done sensibly without weakening the wall in any way . All packing, no matter how tight, will contain spaces and soil can be worked into these to allow the roots of plants set in the wall face to travel right through and into the bank behind. When packing, work soil carefully into the small spaces as you go and be careful not to mix stone with the soil. This process is most easily carried out using dry soil, and it must be undertaken as you build from the bottom, otherwise the first rainfall will wash it out.

Plants that are placed in the face of the wall should be set at the base of vertical joints. These hold a little water and the soil is more likely to be retained here. Soil erosion can be minimised by working pieces of dead turf into the crack with the grass side inward. The turf breaks down in time to produce valuable humus and nutrients for the plants.

A retaining wall may be finished off with flat stones, copestones or turf, depending on your local style and whether or not you want it to provide seating or offer kneeling room for when you do the weeding.

Useful plants for the face of the wall are purple and yellow aubretia, allysum and thyme when facing the sun, or arabis, campanulae and the various saxifrages which will be happier in the shade.

Once plants become established, much of the wall becomes covered and this breaks up what can look initially quite a stark expanse of stone.

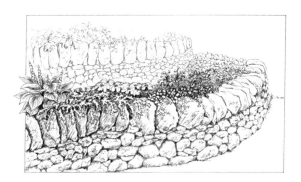

STEPS

The main construction details for dry stone steps were covered earlier; steps are often associated with retaining walls.

In the case of closed steps, firmness is achieved by the binding of each tread under the risers and the side walls above it. Where open steps are built, for example those that project beyond a wall, it is best if the tread of each step is heavy and made of one substantial piece of stone. A similar technique is illustrated for steps against a retaining wall: here the treads are held by the risers and also tied into the retaining wall when both are constructed at the same time.

BARBECUES

Barbecues are best built against, or as part of, another wall, with the site open towards the prevailing wind. When building a barbecue, you can never have too much flat surface around it: plates, food dishes, cooking implements, etc. are best placed on flat surfaces at about waist height, conveniently within reach. Anything placed at ground level is likely to be trodden on, knocked over or broken.

A good supply of flat stone is needed to construct the corners and sides of the cooking area, and you will need a wide slab to hold the fire. Pieces of metal rod can be built into the wall to hold the food while it is cooking. Alternatively you could use a grid which fits within the barbecue sides, raised above the charcoal on suitably shaped stones. It can be lifted out easily for cleaning and storage so that it remains free from rust.

SEATS AND TABLES

Gardens are for pleasure as well as exercise, and when the weather is warm enough, sitting outside is the justification for all your building efforts. Seats and tables can be made freestanding or set against a wall. The main difficulty with free-standing constructions is how to build the pillars that support them: if they are too small, there is a danger that the top slabs will move. Therefore either wide pillars should be built for better stability, or the slabs will have to be drilled and fixed securely to the pillars or through them to the ground below.

Where seats can be recessed into a wall, the stones above hold the slabs in position. The edges of the seat and of tables should be checked for sharp edges, which should be rounded off by careful use of the hammer.

Seats can be built in a similar manner to raised beds, except that the fill in a raised bed is soil rather than solid stone pieces. If either is planned to lie against a house wall you need to check the level of the damp course first. If the feature will bridge it, then prevent any damp from getting into the house wall by inserting a piece of damp-proof membrane or roofing felt.

Select your stone according to the size of the feature that you are building. Unusually shaped stones can often be used in this type of project, though not if their shape compromises the strength of the feature. Free-standing seats or those against walls need good generous slabs to cover their supporting walls. The hearting needs to be well packed and must support the slabs everywhere.

BIRD TABLES, BIRD BATHS AND SUNDIALS

These can be most attractive single features in a garden of any size. They generally involve the construction of a round or square pillar. Normally, a purchased sundial top would be fixed with a little mortar to the completed base; it is important to ensure the alignment is correct. Bird tables need to be topped with a large, flat stone, but to find a similar one with a recess to hold water for a birdbath might be difficult. If a suitable stone cannot be located, some time may be happily spent with a hammer and chisel over a few evenings in creating one.

An alternative base for any of these features would be a broken stone gatepost, set upright in the ground.

Features which are designed to attract birds need to be sited in an open position away from bushes or trees to ensure that cats and vermin are less likely to be attracted by the birds or the food. It will also be a good idea to make them tall enough to deter predators from jumping up on them.

LARGER STRUCTURES

Dry stone work can be successfully used to great effect for buildings in the garden and these can be the focus of attraction for neighbours and friends. Such structures include garden sheds, garages and fruit stores. They are not damp, as may be supposed, but very dry and, because air circulates slowly, tend to provide a much kinder environment for tools and machinery, as well as for stored produce.

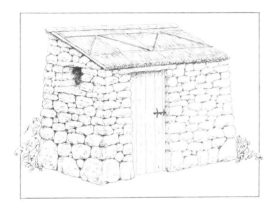

Constructing dry stone buildings is a job for the professional with specialist skills. A good supply of corner stones and lintels is essential, and a method must be devised for tying the roof into the structure. Care should be taken to use a natural roofing medium: artificial material will ruin the effect. Such a building may be expensive, but just think of the pleasure of pricking out your seedlings in a rose-covered stone potting shed.

It is possible – though rare - to build a complete home in dry stone, for example a traditional Scottish blackhouse. These constructions can be adapted to meet modern building regulations. A master craftsman of the Dry Stone Walling Association built a new blackhouse on a green field site on the Isle of Harris in the early 1990s - the first for over a century.

DRY STONE WORK AS FACING

Concrete or block walls in a garden can look so much of an eyesore that the decision is taken to cover them. If there is room to clad, or face, the existing wall with natural stone the effect can be extremely pleasing.

In effect, a single-skinned wall is built in front of the block one. If you do this to any appreciable height, you need to consider putting batter on the wall, beginning farther forward at the base with deeper stone. Unless the original structure has wall ties protruding from it, the use of a little mortar to bind the occasional facing stone to the back wall may be necessary to increase stability. If airbricks or ventilation gratings are present, allowance must be made for these to continue working effectively.

TERRACES AND PATIOS

Although a horizontal feature, terraces and patios have a place here. Natural stone, whether weathered or fresh from the quarry, has a far better texture and appearance than imitation stone flags or concrete slabs.

If you are laying a patio, remove all topsoil and level the ground. Do not dig or loosen the ground too much – a swift rake over will do. Remove projecting stones and, for weed control, lay a membrane. Cover this with a weak, dry mortar mixture on which to set the slabs. If you have a narrow flowerbed between the patio and the house, a slight slope towards this will be useful as the bed will usually be very dry. If not, a slight slope away from the house will ensure that water runs off harmlessly.

Over time, patios become covered in algae, but this can be cleaned with a power washer or hard brush: a water additive may be useful in preventing or slowing the return of the algae.

STONE AND WATER

Stone and water in combination have graced gardens over centuries. Rockeries with tumbling waterfalls mimic upland streams in miniature. These are usually closed systems with pumps to circulate the water.

Although traditionally concrete or puddled clay were used for the watercourses, these often cracked and water was lost. Modern materials, such as butyl rubber liners, have largely taken over; the edges can be effectively concealed under flags or cobbles laid along the edge of the stream or around the pond.

If waterfalls or rapids are to be built, the liner should be brought up behind the facing stones. Where a separate piece of liner is used for the stream or pond above the fall, this liner should be brought well down and in front of the lower position, because too little overlap may result in a leakage. Stone should not be bedded directly on to the liner: this is a case where stone-free, clay-based subsoil is useful.

Where space allows, the liner from a pond can run directly under the flags at the normal water level and then continued to line a depression in the ground. If this extension piece of liner is punctured and filled with peaty soil, it will make a superb bog garden and act as an overflow for the pond in periods of high rainfall.

One final point: never design a system with a large top pond and a smaller bottom one. When the pump is switched on, a large top pond has to be fully filled before the stream and waterfall begin to run: this would deplete the smaller pond and lower the water level considerably.

Where the garden is large enough and a natural stream or ditch exists, this can be dammed with stone and clay to form a pond, or may be bridged using one of the methods described earlier.

Sourcing water-worn stone is less of a problem nowadays, with large cobbles and pebbles available from garden centres and builders' merchants. Removing stones from beaches or rivers is often unlawful and must be avoided.

A simple footbridge over a garden stream can be created with a large slab of stone

OTHER ARTISTIC FEATURES

Natural stone may be used in other ways than construction. A selected single stone may be displayed as an art object, such as a freestanding obelisk. Groupings of stones with interesting shapes may add a focal point to an otherwise bald and unconvincing area. Illustrated is a circular wellhead, built using small stone, which would enhance any cottage garden. Cairns may use up much waste stone in a simple but most appealing way.

ENTRANCES

New homes are often constructed with drives: low walls gracefully curving to lead the eye into the garden add both interest and value to a property. Where these are new, however, you should check planning regulations – there may be restrictions as to height and sight lines, which have to be obeyed.

A wall along one side of a drive may restrict the opening of car doors. A narrow area with a flag laid into the ground on the opposite side of the drive may allow the car to be parked sufficiently far from the wall to allow the opening of the door.

If pillars are to support heavy entrance gates, it will be necessary to find a blacksmith to make sturdy metal uprights with extra long hooks which can be set into the centre of the pillar to take the weight of the gate.

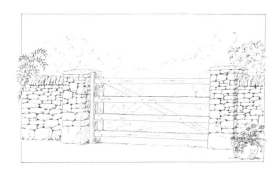

HA-HA

Where a garden adjoins open ground or farmland, there is the opportunity to construct a ha-ha and do away with a fence or hedge. This forms a stockproof barrier and is invisible from the house, thus giving the impression that the garden extends almost endlessly.

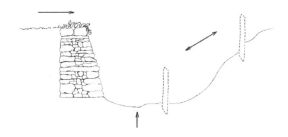

The post and wire fence can be positioned to prevent stock having access to the ha-ha or be placed further back to prevent poaching of the wet ditch

A ha-ha is formed by cutting a wide ditch, with the side nearest the garden almost vertical while the other slopes more gently up towards the field. As you will almost certainly have to construct the whole thing on your own ground, this feature is really only for those with a lot of land. It is usual to include a post and wire fence on the field side to ensure even the most athletic of farm animals are kept at bay, and to prevent excessive poaching of the damp ditch which could result in damage to the footings of the retaining wall. The wire fence would be out of sight from the garden.

CONCLUSION

Almost anyone can achieve sufficient skill with basic techniques to build a satisfying dry stone wall. Of those, many are able to reach a higher degree of competence and a few can truly master the craft.

There is an additional gift which cannot be taught: if you are able to use this toughest of natural materials so that it lies in perfect harmony with its landscape, and create imaginative and pleasing work which combines originality with a certain timeless inevitability in what you build, then you are indeed an artist in stone.

We hope that whether you aspire to walling yourself or wish to learn more about what past and present generations have made, this book has given you an insight into a traditional craft which has probably produced man's greatest impact on the upland landscape in Britain.

Paul Webley, Chairman
& members of
The Dry Stone Walling Association
Of Great Britain
2004

APPENDIX 1

THE DRY STONE WALLING ASSOCIATION OF GREAT BRITAIN

The Dry Stone Walling Association of Great Britain (DSWA) was formed in 1968 from the ever-increasing number of wallers and dykers who had joined the Stewartry of Kirkcudbright Drystane Dyking Committee, which was based in Dumfries & Galloway. Col. F. Rainsford Hannay had formed this group in 1938 to breathe new life into the then dying craft.

Through the efforts of all those involved with the Committee, the enthusiasts who went on to form the national Association and those who later took on the workload in their turn, DSWA has reached the point where it has branches throughout England, Scotland and Wales with associated groups in the USA and a number of other English-speaking countries. It has also established links with like-minded organisations throughout Europe.

The Association works to ensure that the best craftsmanship of the past is preserved, and that the craft has a thriving future. It is the only organisation in Britain, and one of few in the world, which is devoted solely to the craft of building in stone without the use of mortar.

Important objectives of the Association include the furthering of knowledge and understanding of the craft among the general public and, where applicable, working with similar organisations to promote the craft. There are books and leaflets available by post from DSWA, which offer much information to help people find out more about walling. Demonstrations and even competitions may also be seen at county shows wherever DSWA has an active branch.

The Association operates the only national, progressive skills certification scheme – the Craftsman Certification Scheme – which is specific to dry stone walling. Full details of the scheme are available from the DSWA office. There is also an annual register of certificated professional members, which includes details of corporate members who supply stone.

The DSWA is a voluntary organisation and a registered charity. At the time of writing in 2004 there are nineteen branches with over 1,200 members throughout Great Britain. The Association relies on subscription income for its regular running expenses: it constantly seeks donations to enable its work to continue to grow. It also seeks and warmly welcomes new members from all walks of life and of all ages and abilities.

Information about the Association and its work are available on the website, or an information pack can be obtained by sending a stamped, self-addressed envelope to:

**The Dry Stone Walling Association
of Great Britain**
Westmorland County Showground,
Lane Farm,
Crooklands,
Milnthorpe,
Cumbria LA7 7NH.

Website: www.dswa.org.uk

APPENDIX 2

DSWA'S CRAFTSMAN CERTIFICATION SCHEME

The **Dry Stone Walling Association of Great Britain** is a registered charity, founded in 1968 and which encompasses all aspects of the craft in Britain today. Part of the Association's work involves operating a national series of progressive, practical tests leading to the *Master Craftsman Certificate* in dry stone walling. This is a brief outline of the scheme. Those wishing to participate should read the full booklet *DSWA Craftsman Certification Scheme —Introduction and Schedules,* which is available from DSWA.

The scheme, established in the early 1980s, provides recognised skills certification for wallers and dykers giving employers guidance on the ability of the individual. The *Craftsman Certification Scheme* provides a range of tests to meet the needs of today's working waller and dyker in the wide range of work situations: from straight-forward repair work to extensive landscaping projects involving many features.

The *Craftsman Certification Scheme* is designed to ensure candidates achieve the highest standards in the craft. There is a biennial review of the test requirements to ensure the Scheme meets the needs of employers and wallers.

Tests are at four levels:
- **Initial** covers the basics of the craft – the repair a gap;
- **Intermediate** includes the building of a wall with a cheekend or wall head;
- **Advanced** involves both retaining and curved walls;
- **Master Craftsman** covers the building of various structures to a high degree of finish.

In addition, there is a category for *Regional Styles.* Currently there is a test for the Galloway style, open to those of Intermediate Certificate standard. It is anticipated this section of the scheme will grow to encompass further regional styles when there is demand for recognised certification.

In 2004, the Association gained accreditation from the Qualifications and Curriculum Authority for the Intermediate Certificate, and subsequently applied for accreditation of the Initial and Advanced Certificates. This accreditation enables training providers to unlock government funding for courses that include the qualification. Working with Lantra Awards, the Association has devised a system that enables candidates to apply for an accredited certificate: a candidate only takes the one DSWA test and is certificated in the normal manner but can now apply for the additional Lantra Awards certificate. This is not available retrospectively, nor is it available to candidates overseas.

Who carries out the tests?

The Association has a group of Master Craftsman Certificate holders who have been trained in skills assessment and who regularly come together for review of standards. These examiners are present throughout the practical tests and are the only people who can undertake skills assessment for the Scheme.

Who can be tested?

Tests are available to all individuals, whether or not members of the DSWA.

Those on training schemes should commence with the initial test. Those already working in the craft may omit taking the initial test and begin at the intermediate level.

How to apply

Application to be tested forms are available from DSWA and its local branches. The fees include both examination and registration costs.

The DSWA will appoint examiner(s) for all tests sessions. Some DSWA centres operate testing days, the dates of which are published in the DSWA members' magazine, the *Waller & Dyker*.

How tests are arranged and operated

DSWA tests are normally arranged by contacting the local DSWA branch or by seeking details of other registered centres from the DSWA national office. The *Application to be Tested* form gives details of test arrangements.

All tests are conducted under the authority of DSWA examiner(s). Tests are open to all individuals, whether or not they are a member of the Association.

Require advice?

The Association, and its local centres, will advise and where appropriate organise training courses to assist candidates to seek their desired level of certification. Most DSWA branches operate training weekends and practice meets for the beginner or improver. A list of branch contacts is available from the Association or the website.

Lantra Awards can provide details of registered centres offering funded courses.

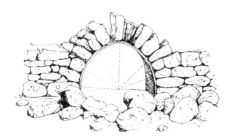

APPENDIX 3

DSWA'S PINNACLE AWARD

The *Pinnacle Award* of the Dry Stone Walling Association commends dry stone walling projects of the highest quality and merit or other noteworthy projects of which dry stone walling comprises the most prominent feature. Only the most outstanding projects incorporating the very best of craftsmanship, innovative design and inspirational use of stone will be eligible for consideration for a Pinnacle Award.

In circumstances where a project falls short of the exacting standards and originality required for a Pinnacle Award yet is, nevertheless, an outstanding example of its type, the Award Panel may grant a *Certificate of Merit* in one of the following categories:

> *Agriculture; Architecture;*
> *Conservation; Forestry;*
> *Landscaping; Public Works;*
> *Historical Restoration;*
> *or other, as appropriate.*

The Award is available for projects only within Great Britain. However, as more organisations supporting the craft are established around the world, it is hoped these will build upon the prestige of the DSWA Pinnacle Award with their own similarly scrutinised awards.

ELIGIBILITY

Projects should be outstanding examples of their type built to the highest standards of craftsmanship. In addition, projects should:

- Be of sufficient individual importance to justify special recognition.
- Be aesthetically pleasing while also displaying the highest standards of craftsmanship.
- Be essentially composed of dry stone walling, although by necessity it is accepted that up to 25% wet walling and/or fencing may be included.
- Be under construction or have been completed within the previous two years.

Uniqueness of design, the waller's skill in its execution, sympathetic use of natural features and imaginative use of available stone are all taken into account when assessing any particular project.

Project managers or others involved with prestigious work that they feel may be eligible for the Pinnacle Award are recommended to contact the DSWA for full Award details and application forms at an early stage in the project.

APPENDIX 4

FUNDING FOR REPAIR AND REBUILDING OF DRY STONE WALLS

The information below is of a general nature to provide background information to help readers to locate relevant funding. It can take time to agree a grant - even when you have located the right one for you - so please be patient. If repair work is due to vehicle or other damage you may have the option of an insurance claim to allow urgent repairs. Some insurers may pay for natural deterioration damage.

NOTE: If seeking grant to assist with the restoration or rebuilding of any dry stone wall or dry-stane dyke, no work should be commenced until details are formally agreed with the relevant grant aiding body.

England: Grant aid for the building and restoration of dry stone walls has been available from a range of sources in recent years. In particular the Ministry of Agriculture, latterly DEFRA, has provided substantial funding under the Countryside Stewardship and the Environmentally Sensitive Areas schemes.

The Countryside Stewardship Scheme has offered a comprehensive menu of walling items, including payments for sourcing replacement stone and working on difficult sites. In its first ten years this scheme alone funded 1,000 miles of walling.

ESAs including the Cotswolds, Dartmoor, South West Peak and North Peak, Pennine Dales and Lake District have offered either capital grants or dry stone walling supplements which have not only encouraged farmers and landowners to improve their walls, but have offered valuable employment opportunities in these areas. The maintenance of stock proof walls is a condition of many ESA schemes, which has ensured the future of varying local styles of wall, and in Cornwall, the West Penwith ESA has offered protection to the very special ancient walls that surround the Bronze Age field systems that characterise the area.

These schemes have resulted in many hundreds of miles of walling being restored. The Countryside Stewardship and Environmentally Sensitive Areas grant schemes closed to new applications in 2004.

Details of current grant schemes may be obtained from local DEFRA offices in England.

In addition, some local authorities can provide assistance for restoration of dry stone walls, particularly those that are not within the scope of DEFRA: you should contact the local authority conservation (or similar) officer to seek information on what may be available.

Wales: The National Assembly for Wales Agriculture Department has operated schemes similar to those in England resulting in the restoration of walls. The Countryside Council for Wales administers *Tir Gofal*, which can provide funding related to wildlife, landscape, archaeology and geology, and for providing opportunities for countryside enjoyment. Dry stone walls and earthbanks, including cloddiau, can qualify for these grants. Details of current schemes can be obtained through local offices of the Agriculture Department and/or Countryside Council for Wales.

Scotland: The Scottish Executive Environment & Rural Affairs Department, Scottish Natural Heritage and The Crofters Commission can provide grants that may include the repair and/or rebuilding of dry stane dykes. In addition, some project-based schemes may find funding available through organisations such as the Greenbelt Trusts. Details of current schemes should be obtained from local offices of the relevant organisation.

APPENDIX 5

DRY STONE WALLS AND WILDLIFE

Britain's flora and fauna owe much to the traditional dry stone walls that provide varied and valuable habitats for a whole range of plants and wild creatures.

How does the hunting stoat move, almost concealed, from one upland valley to the next? Where does the lowland wagtail nest, secure from predators? How can the seed of the fairy foxglove find shelter to germinate and thrive? These and countless other creatures and plants rely upon walls for their survival.

Dry stone walls are, in effect, one huge linear nature reserve and they merit preservation. A little care and imagination when repairing and rebuilding will amply repay the effort and enhance these important habitats, thus helping to protect the great variety of wildlife living in and around them.

Dry stone walls are the dominant field boundaries where rocky outcrops are common, the soil is thin and the climate is too harsh for hedgerows. But some lowland, more fertile regions also boast their share of dry stone walls, often with an earth bank at the bottom. For wildlife, both environments fulfil the same functions as a hedge.

Walls are popular as field boundaries for the shelter that they provide for farm animals. They also provide varied habitats and micro-climates for wild animals.

There is an exposed, wet side and a drier, warmer side. The top is windswept but the bottom sheltered. Inside it can be dry and snug, with perhaps a trickle of water.

FAUNA

Even a well-maintained dry stone wall is not without its holes, nooks and crannies affording hideaways for a myriad of humble insects and their eggs – spiders, woodlice, springtails, millipedes, bees and wasps.

The toad and slow-worm share shelter with the vole, the fieldmouse, the shrew and the hedgehog among the leaf-filled footings and fillings; and the wheatears may lay their clutches of pale blue eggs here if a gap at low level to allow entry is provided.

Higher up, a cavity the size of a house brick offers shelter to the robin or the redstart along the woodland's edge, while in the open farmland, little owls profit from holes deep inside the walls.

Where trees are scarce, an upright copestone acts as a perch or viewpoint, and can form an ideal plucking platform for birds of prey. Bats prefer a stone built "letter box" with a narrow slit immediately beneath the cope of higher walls.

Long, gate-free stretches can be improved for wildlife if smoots or holes are constructed to allow hares and rabbits to pass through. Building a badger gate saves much expense and many hours of work: should these inveterate diggers decide to burrow their own way through they will bring a wall crashing down round their ears!

FLORA

Dry stone walls are wildlife gardens. Lichens - early signs of life - favour the exposed face in the pollution-free countryside. In damp and shaded areas feather and cushion mosses, algae and liverworts clothe the stones, creating tilth and compost for stonecrop, cranesbill, ivy and ferns to gain a foothold.

In lowland Britain, the wall is often the surrogate natural scree or cliff. Wall pennywort, common in some parts of the west, occasionally colonises walls in eastern Britain. The rusty-back fern depends upon them for survival and walls host the polypody, spleenwort, wall rue and many others.

Flora escapees from gardens flourish and add finery to crevices and crannies up and down the country – the ivy-leaved toad flax, Oxford ragwort, Mind-your-own-business and many members of the stonecrop and saxifrage (rock breaker) families.

The typical style of building combining the wall with an earth bank, common in the frost-free areas of the south-west of England and parts of Wales, opens endless possibilities for wild flowers and herbs.

HINTS FOR OWNERS AND WALLERS

To some wildlife, semi-dereliction is more attractive than a tightly-built wall since there are more sheltered spaces and more is covered in soil. However such a state is relatively short lived. Once reduced to less than half its height, a wall's habitat value is considerably reduced. Thus walls need to be sympathetically maintained to provide varied habitats.

Adjacent trees and shrubs can push a wall over so control of these is vital. A strip two feet wide each side should be kept free of vigorous shrubs and trees, and branches near the wall top should be lopped; a trim every few years is usually sufficient. Roots from nearby large trees can be bridged to allow peaceful co-existence.

New stone is often bare and weathering should be encouraged, perhaps by adding a little soil inside or splattering the face with manure. Walls made from existing or reclaimed stone should, where possible, be rebuilt with the weathering and lichen outermost.

SURVEYS

Those who are interested in looking in detail at the habitats in their local dry stone walls will find much help in a set of survey papers available from the Association.

These include sections on wildlife in walls as well as information for surveys of wall lengths and conditions.

The above text is taken from a leaflet published by the Dry Stone Walling Association entitled <u>Dry Stone Walls and Wildlife.</u> Copies available on request.

APPENDIX 6

SPECIFICATIONS & PUBLICATIONS

The Dry Stone Walling Association has developed a range of publications to assist those who are periodically required to specify or design work that incorporates dry stone walling.

The following section contains extracts from the most commonly used leaflets, each of which is available on the DSWA website in a printer-friendly format, or in paper format from the DSWA headquarters (a stamped, self-addressed envelope is appreciated).

Current details of the full range of publications available can be obtained from the website or by post from DSWA.

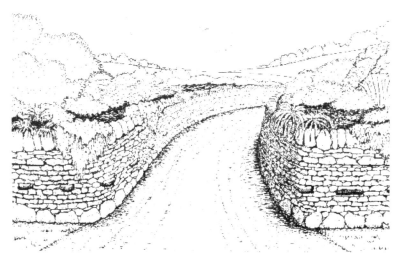

Entrance enhanced with dry stone retaining walls

TECHNICAL SPECIFICATIONS FOR DRY STONE WALLS

PREAMBLE

These notes have been prepared to assist professional decision makers: local authority officers, architects, civil engineers, landscape designers, etc. in drawing up specifications for dry stone walling work. Before giving the most common measurements, a number of important points should be understood:

- There are three key areas in the use of dry stone: *free standing walls* which are by far the most common application of the craft in the United Kingdom; *Load bearing retaining walls* and *domestic structures* particularly houses, barns and ancient monuments. These notes deal with free standing walls of a generally found type. However, there are distinctive regional variations. All walling work should take into consideration the type, stone and style of other dry stone walls close by.

- The specifications relating to load bearing walls are far more complex. A leaflet entitled *Specifications for Simple Retaining Walls* is available from DSWA.

- Matters appertaining to ancient monuments are too variable to be dealt with in short note form and should be handled by discussion between a dry stone walling consultant and the relevant bodies. In all cases, the Association will endeavour to match the inquirer with the best available specialist.

- Dry stone walling is as much an art as a science, and this can occasionally give rise to frustration and misunderstanding among those professionals not fully acquainted with it. Seemingly inconsequential considerations can quite substantially affect the ease of construction and hence, price. A site visit and discussion prior to estimating will almost invariably be necessary for the waller.

- The difference in standards between good and bad work are probably greater than in any other skill. This, combined with the need to recognise the inexperience of those professionals commissioning dry stone walling in judging the quality of the product, makes it essential to obtain the services of a qualified waller and with prestigious work, this is particularly so. Again, the Association will help if asked. To emphasise the point: work should last 100-150 years when carried out by a skilled waller, yet failure in five or less is frequent.

GUIDELINES

- Quite apart from statutory requirement, it is good practice to match walls to those in the immediate area both in style and in materials used. There are distinctive local variations - often in relatively small areas.

- A standard, freestanding wall usually stands 1.4m (4ft 6in) above ground level. Boundary walls (perimeter walls to farms, estates, etc) are more commonly 1.6m (5ft 3in) or more.

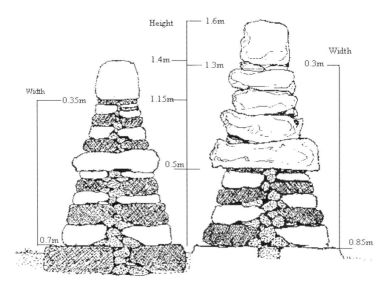

Cross-sections of (left) standard "double" dry stone wall and (right) a Galloway March dyke.
(Measurements are as a guide only)

- A wall may be more or less any height, *providing* this is reflected in the base width.

- A foundation course is required for all work not built on rock.

- When restoring walls after ground disturbance (e.g. pipeline works) care should be taken to backfill with subsoil or similar material avoiding organic matter, and to follow this up by mechanical compacting.

- When dismantling walls with a view to re-using the stone, it is imperative that no soil or other foreign material whatever is mixed with the stone which is retained. This usually inhibits the use of machinery. The best course of action is to place a mechanical digger bucket against the wall and hand load. Aim to keep the various components separate (i.e. top stones, through stones, building stones, etc).

- It is important to bear in mind that the waller can obviously only work with the material supplied. Surprisingly, it is not at all uncommon for the commissioning body to provide a specification similar to the drawings above, yet supply stone that makes faithful execution of that specification impossible. Some stone can be coursed; some is only suitable for random walling. Where an *exact* reproduction is not essential, allowances must be made according to materials and conditions.

TECHNICAL SPECIFICATIONS FOR SIMPLE RETAINING WALLS

PREAMBLE

The following notes form part of a series of technical specification leaflets designed to give guidance on particular aspects of the craft of dry stone walling. Before giving detailed guidelines, several points should be understood.

- Stone supplied must be clean. Dismantling of existing structures should be done by hand.
- The difference between good and bad work is probably greater than any other skill. It is essential to obtain the services of a qualified waller, particularly with prestigious projects. DSWA operates the only tiered, national, practical skills certification scheme in dry stone walling.
- The waller can obviously only work with the stone supplied: specify a style/design that can be built with available material.
- Where possible, match stone type and style to the tradition of the area.

GUIDELINES

For practical purposes, retaining walls may be divided into two types: the first is "domestic" walls, under 1.5m in height and not subject to heavy loading such as field walls with a substantial difference in ground level on either side, garden retaining walls or ha-ha. These notes refer to these "domestic" walls.

The second type are fully load-bearing walls and a civil engineer should be consulted at all times. However, dry stone in civil engineering work is a very narrow field. DSWA Master Craftsman Certificate holders who regularly undertake large-scale contract work would assist engineers in designing safe sections.

A retaining wall may be formed by building a standard wall with carefully laid back-fill. However, in some regions many retaining walls are single skin only, whereby only the outer face is built up, back filling as work proceeds.

There are many variations with retaining walls, but the following points are almost universal.

- In forming a new retaining wall, the banking must be cut back to a distance at least equal to half the height of the finished wall. If the material behind the wall is loose or liable to slumping, cut back further and/or slope the face of the bank away from the wall.

- The foundations must be hard and level. Insert a foundation course in all instances. Two-thirds of the width of the foundation stones should lie within the line of the subsequent structure. The width of the base of the wall is usually one-third to one-half of the finished height.

- The batter (inward slope) should be 1:6 for maximum strength and longevity; greater if there is any doubt about the likely effect of lateral pressure. Such pressures are greatly increased by water saturation in wet spells, with wall failures increasing markedly at such times. Low walls can be built with less batter, sometimes almost vertically, but there may be a pay-off in terms of durability.

Sections through a Yorkshire-style (far right) retaining wall and a Scottish-style retaining dyke

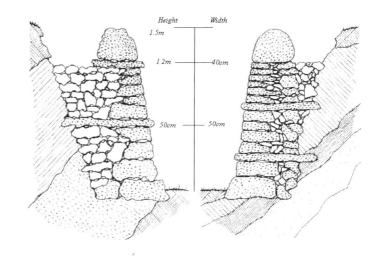

- Lay throughstones as frequently as their availability permits, choosing stones that tie back as far as possible. Ideally, they should be tied into the bank behind, with extra excavation if necessary.

- Particular attention should be paid to the face stones, so as to ensure that each one runs into the wall and not along its length. It is important to use as large face stones as possible. The bedding planes should be parallel to the base.

- Use selected, heavy copes (top stones) particularly if the wall is backfilled to the top. Occasionally, a wall is topped with large, heavy stones laid flat to be level with ground on the higher side.

- Dry stone walls are free draining. However, where the hearting is solid (where soil has been incorporated in garden terracing), or where crushed waste is employed, construct weep holes for drainage at 2-3m intervals, more frequently where water is a problem. It is not uncommon to find water from rock strata, field drains, etc when cutting back the bank, and this should be taken away by constructing drains or drainage channels in the foundation to prevent water erosion.

TECHNICAL SPECIFICATIONS FOR CORNISH & STONE HEDGES

PREAMBLE

These notes have been prepared to assist professional decision makers: local authorities, architects, civil engineers, landscape designers, etc, in drawing up specifications for dry stone work which covers a flexible subsoil or stone core, These constructions are found typically in Cornwall where they are called Cornish _hedges,_ or stone _hedges,_

- There are three key areas in the use of dry stone: _free-standing walls_ which are by far the most common application of the craft in the United Kingdom; _load-bearing retaining walls_ and _domestic structures_ particularly houses, barns and ancient monuments. There is a separate leaflet dealing with standard dry stone and Galloway style walls. These notes deal with stone-faced hedge banks, called Cornish hedges or stone hedges. Some of these were built in the Bronze Age, and others are mediaeval: the details of rebuilding these should be handled by discussion between the actual hedger and English Heritage.

- Cornish hedging is as much an inherited skill as a science, and this can occasionally give rise to frustration and misunderstanding among those professionals not fully acquainted with hedging in Cornwall. Ignorance and omission of small details in specification is reflected both in the building costs and in the integrity of the hedge i.e. a site visit and discussion prior to estimating will invariably be necessary for the hedger.

- The difference in standards between good and bad work is probably greater than many other skills. Both those commissioning Cornish hedging and those doing the work need to be properly qualified. The DSWA will help if asked.

Most hedging contracts are tendered contracts, with an inadequate, and often incorrect, specification. With the cheapest quote usually being accepted, an inferior job inevitably results. The DSWA believes from long experience that poor supervision limited by a bad specification results in hedges which often require rebuilding. The DSWA may be able to assist with standard clauses.

GUIDELINES

- Quite apart from any statutory requirement, it is good practice to match building methods and stone to those in the immediate area. The commissioning body should specify both the nature and source of stone. It should identify a section of nearby hedge which illustrates the hedging pattern for the hedger to follow.

- The typical, freestanding Cornish or stone hedge stands about 1.5m (4ft 6in) above ground level, and varies in height from less than lm (3ft) up to over 3m (10ft).

- The base width is normally equal to the hedge height, and the width of the hedge top is equal to half the base width. Exceptionally, stone hedges are built extra wide to store stones cleared from the field within the thickness of the hedge.

- Where restoring Cornish or stone hedges after ground disturbance (e.g. gas or water pipelines) care should be taken to backfill with subsoil avoiding vegetable matter, and to follow this up by mechanical compaction.

- The lower half of every hedge is concavely curved with the upper surface of the grounders set at the traditional angle (batter) made by the shaft to the blade of a Cornish shovel, about 30-35 degrees for the typical 1.5m hedge, less for lower and more for higher hedges. Where cattle are enclosed, the upper half of the hedge has parallel vertical sides. With sheep, the top quarter often has an outwards batter of 25-75mm and/or coping stones may be used. In other circumstances the upper quarter of the hedge has parallel sides. The usual lifespan of a hedge with straight or convex batter is less than one-tenth that of a similar hedge with the correct concave batter (typically more than 150 years).

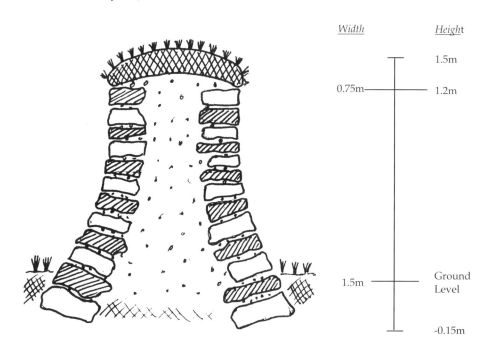

Width   Height

1.5m

0.75m — 1.2m

1.5m — Ground Level

-0.15m

Cross-section of standard stone hedge showing the concave face
(Measurements are as a guide only)

- Stones are to diminish in size for each course in vertical sequence. Vertical joints on every course are staggered by at least 100mm (4") for stone laid horizontally, and 25mm (1") for stone laid vertically. Herringbone is laid with the stones, usually slate, individually interlocking. Stones should be typically coursed with their bedding plane parallel with the way laid, and with their longest side set at right angles to the line of hedge. With the exception of the top course, all stones to be load-bearing and to be so laid as to be incapable of individual extraction.

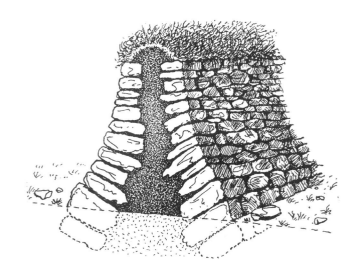

- For Cornish hedges, the fill to be of damp granular or shale-like subsoil type (e.g. rab, growan, shillet) without topsoil or other vegetable matter, compacted in 150mm layers, fortified with surplus stones. As the Cornish hedge is built, a small sliver of turf the size of a man 's hand, and less than 40mm thick, is laid between the stones every third course, and spaced the same distance apart horizontally. The turf is dug from the land alongside the hedge. For stone hedges, the fill comprises random stones, laid interlocking.

- Cornish and stone hedges are built in a variety of patterns, largely dependant on the type of stone. Patterns include different ways of alternating horizontal, vertical and herringbone (Jack & Jill) courses. Coping stones under the top course are sometimes used against hill breeds of sheep and are essential for deer.

- For Cornish hedges, to allow for settlement, the top is domed with fill to a middle height of 30% of the top width, and covered with turf 150m (6") thick completely overlapping the top course. Stone hedges are usually capped with a course of stones laid vertically but may be finished off as for a Cornish hedge.

- Finally the work should be fenced appropriately to the livestock kept.

SPECIFICATION FOR SINGLE WALLS OR BOULDER DYKES

PREAMBLE
The following notes form part of a series of technical leaflets designed to give guidance on particular aspects of the craft of dry stone walling. This leaflet should be used in conjunction with Technical Specifications for Dry Stone Walls. Before giving detailed guidelines, several points should be understood.

- The difference between good and bad work is probably greater than with any other skill. It is essential to retain the services of a qualified waller, particularly with prestigious projects. DSWA operates the only tiered, national, practical skills certification scheme.

- Most contracts are tendered with the cheapest quote usually being accepted. In dry stone walling speed directly affects quality so that special care is needed to assess the skill of the dyker/waller and also to monitor the quality of the wall during construction.

- Wherever possible, the type of stone and the style of building should be matched to the tradition of the area.

- The dyker or waller can only work with the stone supplied. If a particular style is required, then material suitable for that style must be available.

- Stone supplied to the dyker or waller must be clean. Contractors undertaking the dismantling of existing structures should do so by hand if at all possible.

A single wall or dyke is only a single stone thick, whereas the more common double wall consists of two stone walls to form the faces, with small stones to fill the gap, and throughstones and topstones bridging the two face walls to hold them together.

Single or boulder dykes form only a small proportion of all walls, but can be common in some localities where most of the stones are very large boulders.

They are almost invariably built of field clearance stone as opposed to quarried material, and the rock type is usually igneous, most commonly granite. Single dykes are therefore usually associated with upland areas, particularly in Scotland, but also in parts of Wales, the north of England and the West Country.

Compared with a double wall, a well built boulder wall has some distinct advantages: the boulders in the bottom layer present a large and almost continuous stone surface to the ground giving excellent resistance to settlement; a boulder wall is quicker to build and faster to repair. However, building a boulder dyke requires special skills and wherever possible it is sensible to use a DSWA certificated craftsman who is experienced in this particular style of construction. Because the stones in boulder walls are often very large, a team of two or more wallers, and perhaps mechanical aids, will often be necessary.

GUIDELINES

- Single walls do not have a formal foundation course of large flat stones. However, as with all dry stone work, the top 15cm or so of top soil, together with any organic material, must be removed to provide a level, firm surface. Soft spots should be improved by ramming waste stone into them.

- The first layer should consist of the largest stones laid with their flattest face on the bottom. Each must touch its neighbour and be pinned with rough wedge-shaped stones driven beneath to prevent any movement. It is most important not to use large pins which will bear a significant part of the weight of the wall since this will lead to premature settlement and failure of that section of wall.

- The boulders can be as large as can be manoeuvred. If they are very large, regular and their width is sufficient, it is permissible to lay them along the wall.

- Second and subsequent layers are laid across the wall in the grooves formed by the lower layer. They will break the joints. The stones should be laid so that they do not rock on a dome. No stone should project beyond the stone below, so that an "A" shape section is maintained.

- Similarly, the top stones and the layer immediately below should not be wider than the next lower layer.

- Top stones are traditionally heavy, in keeping with the look of the rest of the wall/dyke.

- The wall should be carefully pinned with sharp-edged, wedge-shaped stones, preferably freshly broken so their roughness keys into the wall. There should not be more than one pin for each hole, and they should not protrude proud of the wall's surface.

- Very large, long stones may be laid upright, or at a slight angle, through several courses or even from top to bottom of the wall.

- One style of single wall uses wide, flat stones laid on end, rather than round boulders. This is only done with hard rocks since sedimentary material (such as sandstone) must be laid with the bedding plane horizontal to prevent weathering. In this style, the stones are again laid in the gaps between the stones of the lower layer, but the overlap is greater so that they are well supported. The wall is stronger than a round boulder wall.

- Whatever the overall height of the wall, the base width should be half the total height.

- In some regions, turf topping to a single dyke/wall is common.

SPECIFICATIONS FOR COTSWOLD OOLITIC LIMESTONE WALLS

PREAMBLE

The following notes are part of a series of technical leaflets designed to give guidance on particular aspects of the craft of dry stone walling. This leaflet should be used in conjuction with *Technical Specifications for Dry Stone Walls.* Before giving detailed guidelines for Cotswold walls, several points should be emphasised.

- The difference between good and bad work is probably greater in dry stone walling than with any other skill. It is essential to retain the services of a qualified waller, particularly with prestigious projects. DSWA operates the only tiered, national practical skills certification scheme.
- Most contracts are tendered, with the cheapest quote usually being accepted. In dry stone walling, speed directly affects quality. Special care is needed to assess the skill of the waller and also to monitor the quality of the wall during construction.
- Wherever possible, the type of stone and the style of building should be matched to the tradition of the area.
- The waller can only work with the stone supplied. If a particular style is required, then material suitable for that style must be available.
- Where walls are dismantled mechanically a lot of existing Cotswold stone is damaged and made unfit for reuse.

Cotswold walls made of oolitic limestone are one of the most noticeable features of the southern English landscape with stone varying from the golden colour of freshly quarried stone through a mellow honey to the greyer, weathered colour of much older walls.

When freshly quarried, the stone is soft and easily worked but suffers from its small size and a tendency to "blow" or flake when attacked by the weather.

A characteristic of traditional Cotswold walling is the placing of stone with its length along the wall. This ensures a long neat face but the practice, which is frowned upon in most walling areas, is felt to reduce strength in the finished wall.

As the stone is small, the rate of work of the waller is slow and prices reflect this.

Little settlement occurs in Cotswold walls as the soil is thin and the trench excavated for foundations often reaches to rock only 80-100mm below the soil surface.

Field walls are normally a little more than one metre high, including the cope, and may be built without throughstones although three-quarter-throughs are regularly used to tie the faces together.

GUIDELINES

- Cotswold walls are built on footings set in a shallow trench which is often no deeper than 100mm and with the footings placed to give a base width of 600mm. The largest suitable stones are chosen to form this foundation course and must be well pinned with rough wedge-shaped pieces from the inside edge to prevent movement and to bear the weight of the wall. Each stone used should touch those next to it and be chosen to project back into the wall as far as possible.

- The centre of the foundation course should be filled with broken stone which should be carefully placed to ensure that any wedges are not forced out as each new course is added.

- The main body of the wall is made up of two skins of coursed stones and a centre/heart carefully filled with broken stone. The face stones are normally laid length along the wall with their inner faces wedged to be level or slightly above the outer face. This sheds water allowing the stone to dry out, reducing chemical and physical weathering. The Cotswold waller makes greater use of his hammer on new stone, removing bumps to produce a dressed, even face to the wall with stones locked tightly together.

- Where stones large enough to project well into the wall are to be found, they are laid to overlap in the middle of the wall, projecting three-quarters of the way through above the filling. The stones are placed at approximately half-height of the wall.

- Batter: the amount by which each course is placed in from the one below it is almost imperceptible in Cotswold walls, with the top width of the wall being three-quarters to two-thirds of the base width.

- Building of the main body of the wall, which starts 600mm wide at the base, finishes at 900mm high and a width of 375mm. This top is then bridged with upright rough tops (combers) which provide weight and stability to prevent the wall from opening. In some areas use is made of mortar in the top, but this is not recommended.

- The building of wallheads presents a problem and the usual methods of single cross-ties sitting on two long stones tying into the wall can rarely be used except near the top of the wall. To overcome this, a two-on-three technique, rather than one-on-two, is used. Where new stone is available this stone is often very carefully dressed by the waller.

A BRIEF GUIDE TO THE INSPECTION OF DRY STONE WALLING WORK

PREAMBLE

These notes are designed to give guidance on particular aspects of dry stone walling. They come from a whole series of DSWA leaflets which have been written to help professional decision makers such as local authority officers, architects, landscape designers, land agents, etc., to judge the merits of different tenders, to draw up specifications for dry stone work and to assess the quality of the work that is being or has been done.

The notes give guidance on what to look for in dry stone walls so you have value for money and know that they have been built to last. They have been produced in response to requests to DSWA over the years concerning the quality of work that has already been carried out.

Before detailing guidelines for the inspection of work, it is important to appreciate that even a good craftsman needs to be supplied with suitable conditions in order to produce a good job. The final result is the product of the craftsman, the stone and the land.

- There is an enormous difference between the best and the worst workmanship, a qualitative gap probably greater than for any other skill. It is therefore essential to employ a qualified professional and the DSWA will supply its list of professional members on request. The DSWA operates a scheme of skills certification involving careful testing. The level of qualification attained by each professional member is indicated in the listings.

- The earth or rock sub-foundation on which the stone wall is to be built needs to be level, firm, and at a depth specified by the waller, unless he is to undertake this himself as part of the contract.

- It is necessary to have clean material, uncontaminated by soil or anything else, delivered to hand at the rate required.

- It is essential, if a specific style is required, for stone to be provided that enables faithful execution of the specification. The stone must be sound, long-lasting, of suitable size and range of sizes with sufficient foundation stones, throughstones, fillings and top stones.

- No mortar should be used unless specified for special reasons.

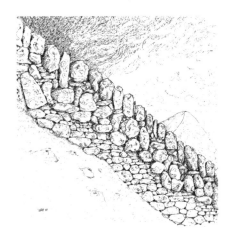

A Galloway dyke on steep ground

GUIDELINES

- The wall should be inspected during the construction as well as after completion.

- The size of the wall should meet the minimum dimensions given in the specifications and should conform to the specified style. A leaflet *Technical Specifications for Dry Stone Walls* is available from DSWA and describes the specification. The foundations (the initial course upon which the subsequent structure is built) should consist of large, flat stones which should each reach at least a third of the way across the wall. In some areas it is normal for the foundations to project some 50-100mm beyond the base of each face of the wall. If an inspection is carried out during construction, which is recommended, foundation stones should not move appreciably when walked on.

- Stand a few metres away and look directly at each face. There should be no "running joints", that is the stones should be bonded as with brickwork, with a stone across each joint in the course below. However, in some stonework, two small face stones are often laid upon each other to level up to an adjacent larger stone, causing an apparent short running joint, which is permissible. Stones should be graded with the larger in the lower part of the wall, except where the local style differs.

- All stones should be placed to touch all their neighbouring stones so that there is no room for movement. There should be little or no front pinning: this is the procedure of wedging the building stones on the outer face using small stones pushed in from the front. This, unfortunately, is frequently done in an attempt to disguise poor workmanship when the stones are not laid tightly enough. It should not be possible to move any stone by hand.

- The fillings, or internal packing of small stones, should be firm with no spaces for settling or movement of the face stones inwards. The fillings are best inspected during the construction since it is impossible to examine the internal structure after completion. However, a check can be made on the thoroughness or otherwise of the packing by a sharp blow to the face of the wall. The force used should not be severe; there should be little or no inward movement and no sound of settling stone from within.

- Examine the throughstones. If at all possible they should be cut to project not more than 50-75mm beyond the face of the wall, particularly if any stock have access. Any sharp edges should have been blunted. Look beneath the throughstone to check that the top surfaces of the supporting stones are secure against the bottom surface of the throughstone. There should be at least the specified number of throughstones.

- Kneel down and look along the face of the wall. It should be absolutely straight and true along its length without waviness, bulges or overhangs. Look down the wall from the top: the batter (the angle of taper to the vertical) should be even from top to bottom.

- The coverstones are flat stones similar to throughstones which cross the width of the wall at the top, immediately below the copestones (these are not used in all regional styles).

- The upper line of the top stones or copestones should be completely level unless there is a regional variation to this. If laid in vertical style, all should be vertical. If laid at an angle, all copestones should be laid at the same angle. Give the copes a firm, sideways push – they should be completely rigid. The copestones, like coverstones, should cross the width of the wall and touch the tops of the stones in the face at both sides. The copestones should not project beyond the faces of the wall. The pinning – small stones wedged in the gaps between the copes – should be pushed in flush to the main structure.

- General: the top of the wall should not have sharp peaks and troughs when following undulating ground, but gently follow the contours. On gentle slopes, the courses should be parallel with the ground; on sharper gradients the courses should be laid horizontally and stepped. Stand back and look at the finished product. There should be distinct lines: foundations, throughstones, coverbands (where used) and top or copestones.

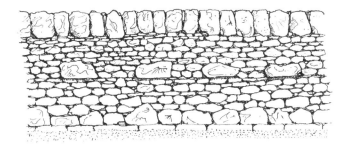

DISPUTES

In the case of disputes involving dry stone work, the Association can provide a list of recommended assessors who can undertake inspection. Details are available from the Association, without obligation.

APPENDIX 7

A BRIEF GLOSSARY

Terms commonly used in the craft of dry stone walling and dyking, some of which appear in this booklet.

"A" Frame: is a wooden or metal frame used as a guide when building.

Batter: This is the inward taper of the wall from base to top.

Consumption dyke: Wall built with stone to clear the land and which is especially wide. Also called "clearance wall" and "accretion wall".

Copestones: the top stones, the stones along the top of the wall to give weight and protection. Also called "cams", "tops", "toppers".

Course: Horizontal layer of stones placed in a wall.

Coverband: Large flat stones placed across width at top of wall in some areas to form base for the copestones.

Double, doubling or double dyking: term used for a dry stone wall built with two faces of stones, packed with hearting between.

Dyking: Scottish term for a dry stone wall.

End-stone: large cope stone topping a cheekend or wallhead.

Foundation: the first layer of large stones in the base of the wall, also called "footing" or "found".

Galf stones: Three-quarter throughstones laid on alternate courses so that tails overlap in centre of wall.

Galloway Dyke: wall or dyke with lower third "doubled", upper two thirds in single walling.

Gap or gapping: a breach in a dry stone wall. Gapping is the repair of same and the "gapper" is the waller or dyker who carries out the repair.

Hearting: the small stones used as packing in a double wall.

Pinnings or pins: small, usually tapering stones used from inside the wall to wedge building stones firmly in place.

Retaining wall: dry stone wall built into the cut face of a bank to prevent the soil from moving down the slope.

Single dyke: wall built with single stones going the width of the wall.

Throughstones: heavy, large stones placed at regular intervals along the wall to tie the two sides together. For three-quarter throughs see "Galf Stones".

Trace walling: incorrect placing of stones with their length along face of wall rather than placing into the wall for strength.

Wallhead: Vertical end to a length of wall. Also called "cheekend".

Watershot: Setting of building stones with outer edge slightly lower than centre.